The "Teaching of English" Series

*General Editor*—Sir Henry Newbolt

# NINE MODERN PLAYS

No. 103

JOHN GALSWORTHY

*From a pen-drawing by*
*E. Heber Thompson*

# NINE
# MODERN PLAYS

Selected and Edited by
JOHN HAMPDEN

THOMAS NELSON & SONS, Ltd.
LONDON, EDINBURGH, AND NEW YORK

*First published November 1926*
*Reprinted March 1927 ; August 1927*

# CONTENTS

Application for leave to act these plays in public must be made as follows:

1. For *Riders to the Sea* by J. M. Synge, *The Bishop's Candlesticks* by N. McKinnel, *The Philosopher of Butterbiggins* by H. Chapin, *The Price of Coal* by H. Brighouse, and *The Old Bull* by B. Gilbert, to Messrs. Samuel French, 26 Southampton Street, London, W.C.2.

2. For *The Poetasters of Ispahan* by Clifford Bax, to Messrs. Peters, 20 Essex Street, London, W.C.2.

3. For *The Little Man* by John Galsworthy, and *The Rehearsal* by M. Baring, to The Collection Bureau, The Society of Authors, 11 Gower Street, London, W.C.1.

4. For *Allison's Lad* by B. M. Dix, to Mr. R. Golding Bright, 20 Green Street, Leicester Square, London, W.C.2.

For further information regarding acting fees, see pages 229 *et seq.* of this book.

# A BOOK OF MODERN PLAYS

## PREFACE

THE aim of this little volume is to present a varied collection of modern one-act plays, ranging from tragedy to farce, which will appeal to the upper forms of secondary and continuation schools, to play-reading circles, and to all who are interested in drama. The plays have been chosen as particularly suitable, not only for reading and study, but for amateur production by players young or old, and all except two are very simple to stage.

The editor wishes to express his thanks to the following authors and publishers for permission to include their plays in this book :

Mr. Norman McKinnel and Messrs. Samuel French for *The Bishop's Candlesticks* ; the representatives of the late Harold Chapin and Messrs. Gowans and Gray, the publishers of the play as a separate booklet, for *The Philosopher of Butterbiggins* ; the Honourable Maurice Baring and Messrs. W. Heinemann, Ltd., for *The Rehearsal* ; Mr. Harold Brighouse for the manuscript of *The Price of Coal*, as well as to Messrs. Gowans and Gray who publish the Lanarkshire version of the play separately ; Mrs. Flebbe (Miss B. M. Dix) and Messrs. Henry Holt and Co. for *Allison's Lad* ; Mr. Bernard Gilbert and Messrs. Samuel French for *The Old Bull* ; Mr. John Galsworthy and Messrs. Duckworth and Co., Ltd., for *The Little Man* ; Mr. Clifford Bax and Messrs. Henderson for *The Poetasters of Ispahan* ; and the owners of the copy-

right and Messrs. Allen and Unwin for *Riders to the Sea*,
by J. M. Synge.*

The editor also desires to acknowledge gratefully his
indebtedness to Dr. Richard Wilson, for endless patience
in the business of copyright arrangements ; to the invalu-
able lending libraries of the British Drama League and
the Village Drama Society, without which the task of
selecting the plays would have been much more difficult ;
and to his wife, for constant help and criticism in this
as in so many other enterprises.

J. H.

* Messrs. Allen and Unwin also publish the following plays by
the same author : *The Shadow of the Glen*, *The Well of the Saints*,
*The Tinker's Wedding*, *The Playboy of the Western World*, *Deirdre
of the Sorrows*.

# THE BISHOP'S CANDLESTICKS

## By Norman McKinnel

Originally produced at the Duke of York's Theatre on August 24, 1901, with the following cast:

| | |
|---|---|
| THE BISHOP . . . . . | . Mr. A. E. George. |
| THE CONVICT . . . . | . Mr. Norman McKinnel. |
| PERSOMÉ (*the Bishop's sister, a widow*) . . . . . . . | . Miss Nannie Griffin. |
| MARIE . . . . . . | . Miss Constance Walton. |
| SERGEANT OF GENDARMES . | . Mr. Frank Woolfe. |

It was revived at the Kingsway Theatre on Friday December 20, 1907, with the following cast:

| | |
|---|---|
| THE BISHOP . . . . . . | . Mr. Henry Vibart. |
| THE CONVICT . . . . | . Mr. Lemmon Warde. |
| PERSOMÉ . . . . . . | . Miss Evelyn Hall. |
| MARIE . . . . . . | . Miss Maud Stewart. |
| SERGEANT OF GENDARMES . | . Mr. Douglas Gordon. |

TIME.—The beginning of the nineteenth century.
PLACE.—France, about thirty miles from Paris.

# THE BISHOP'S CANDLESTICKS

SCENE.—*The kitchen of the* BISHOP'S *cottage. It is plainly but substantially furnished. Doors* R. *and* L. *and* L. C. *Window* R. C. *Fireplace with heavy mantelpiece down* R. *Oak settle with cushions behind door* L. C. *Table in window* R. C. *with writing materials and crucifix (wood). Eight-day clock* R. *of window. Kitchen dresser, with cupboard to lock, down* L. *Oak dining-table* R. C. *Chairs, books, etc. Winter wood scene without. On the mantelpiece are two very handsome candlesticks, which look strangely out of place with their surroundings.*

[MARIE *and* PERSOMÉ *discovered.* MARIE *stirring some soup on the fire.* PERSOMÉ *laying the cloth, etc.*]

*Persomé.* Marie, isn't the soup boiling yet ?

*Marie.* Not yet, Madam.

*Persomé.* Well, it ought to be. You haven't tended the fire properly, child.

*Marie.* But, Madam, you yourself made the fire up.

*Persomé.* Don't answer me back like that. It is rude.

*Marie.* Yes, Madam.

*Persomé.* Then don't let me have to rebuke you again.

*Marie.* No, Madam.

*Persomé.* I wonder where my brother can be. [*Looking at the clock*] It is after eleven o'clock and no sign of him. Marie !

*Marie.* Yes, Madam.

*Persomé.* Did Monseigneur the Bishop leave any message for me ?

*Marie.* No, Madam.

*Persomé.* Did he tell you where he was going?

*Marie.* Yes, Madam.

*Persomé* [*imitating*]. "Yes, Madam." Then why haven't you told me, stupid!

*Marie.* Madam didn't ask me.

*Persomé.* But that is no reason for your not telling me, is it?

*Marie.* Madam said only this morning I was not to chatter, so I thought——

*Persomé.* Ah, mon Dieu, you thought! Ah! it is hopeless.

*Marie.* Yes, Madam.

*Persomé.* Don't keep saying "Yes, Madam," like a parrot, nincompoop.

*Marie.* No, Madam.

*Persomé.* Well, where did Monseigneur say he was going?

*Marie.* To my mother's, Madam.

*Persomé.* To your mother's indeed! And why, pray?

*Marie.* Monseigneur asked me how she was, and I told him she was feeling poorly.

*Persomé.* You told him she was feeling poorly, did you? And so my brother is to be kept out of his bed, and go without his supper, because you told him she was feeling poorly. There's gratitude for you!

*Marie.* Madam, the soup is boiling!

*Persomé.* Then pour it out, fool, and don't chatter. [MARIE *about to do so.*] No, no; not like that. Here, let me do it, and do you put the salt cellars on the table—the silver ones.

*Marie.* The silver ones, Madam?

*Persomé.* Yes, the silver ones. Are you deaf as well as stupid?

*Marie.* They are sold, Madam.

*Persomé.* Sold! [*with horror*] sold! Are you mad? Who sold them? Why were they sold?

*Marie.* Monseigneur the Bishop told me this afternoon while you were out to take them to Monsieur Gervais, who has often admired them, and sell them for as much as I could.

*Persomé.* But you had no right to do so without asking me.

*Marie* [*with awe*]. But, Madam, Monseigneur the Bishop told me.

*Persomé.* Monseigneur the Bishop is a—ahem! but —but what can he have wanted with the money?

*Marie.* Pardon, Madam, but I think it was for Mère Gringoire.

*Persomé.* Mère Gringoire indeed. Mère Gringoire! What, the old witch who lives at the top of the hill, and who says she is bedridden because she is too lazy to do any work? And what did Mère Gringoire want with the money, pray?

*Marie.* Madam, it was for the rent. The bailiff would not wait any longer, and threatened to turn her out to-day if it were not paid, so she sent little Jean to Monseigneur to ask for help, and——

*Persomé.* Oh, mon Dieu! It is hopeless, hopeless. We shall have nothing left. His estate is sold, his savings have gone. His furniture, everything. Were it not for my little dot we should starve! And now my beautiful—beautiful [*sob*] salt cellars. Ah, it is too much, too much [*she breaks down crying*].

*Marie.* Madam, I am sorry. If I had known——

*Persomé.* Sorry, and why, pray? If Monseigneur the Bishop chooses to sell his salt cellars he may do so, I suppose. Go and wash your hands, they are disgracefully dirty.

*Marie.* Yes, Madam [*going towards* R.].

[*Enter the* BISHOP, C.]

*Bishop.* Ah! how nice and warm it is in here. It is worth going out in the cold for the sake of the comfort of coming in.

[PERSOMÉ *has hastened to help him off with his
coat, etc.* MARIE *has dropped a deep courtesy.*

*Bishop.* Thank you, dear. [*Looking at her*] Why,
what is the matter? You have been crying. Has
Marie been troublesome, eh? [*shaking his finger at
her*]. Ah!

*Persomé.* No, it wasn't Marie—but—but——

*Bishop.* Well, well, you shall tell me presently.
Marie, my child, run home now; your mother is better.
I have prayed with her, and the doctor has been.
Run home! [MARIE *putting on cloak and going.*] And,
Marie, let yourself in quietly in case your mother is
asleep.

*Marie.* Oh, thanks, thanks, Monseigneur.

[*She goes to door* C.; *as it opens the snow drives in.*

*Bishop.* Here, Marie, take my comforter, it will keep
you warm. It is very cold to-night.

*Marie.* Oh no, Monseigneur! [*shamefacedly*].

*Persomé.* What nonsense, brother; she is young,
she won't hurt.

*Bishop.* Ah, Persomé, you have not been out, you
don't know how cold it has become. Here, Marie, let
me put it on for you [*does so*]. There! Run along,
little one.                                [*Exit* MARIE, C.

*Persomé.* Brother, I have no patience with you.
There, sit down and take your soup, it has been waiting ever so long. And if it is spoilt, it serves you right.

*Bishop.* It smells delicious.

*Persomé.* I'm sure Marie's mother is not so ill that
you need have stayed out on such a night as this. I
believe those people *pretend* to be ill just to have the
Bishop call on them. They have no thought of the
Bishop!

*Bishop.* It is kind of them to want to see me.

*Persomé.* Well, for my part, I believe that charity
begins at home.

*Bishop.* And so you make me this delicious soup.
You are very good to me, sister.

*Persomé.* Good to you, yes! I should think so. I should like to know where you would be without me to look after you. The dupe of every idle scamp or lying old woman in the parish.

*Bishop.* If people lie to me they are poorer, not I.

*Persomé.* But it is ridiculous; you will soon have nothing left. You give away everything, everything ! ! !

*Bishop.* My dear, there is so much suffering in the world, and I can do so little [*sighs*], so very little.

*Persomé.* Suffering, yes; but you never think of the suffering you cause to those who love you best, the suffering you cause to me.

*Bishop* [*rising*]. You, sister dear. Have I hurt you? Ah, I remember you had been crying. Was it my fault? I didn't mean to hurt you. I am sorry.

*Persomé.* Sorry. Yes. Sorry won't mend it. Humph! Oh, do go on eating your soup before it gets cold.

*Bishop.* Very well, dear [*sits*]. But tell me——

*Persomé.* You are like a child, I can't trust you out of my sight. No sooner is my back turned than you get that little minx Marie to sell the silver salt cellars.

*Bishop.* Ah, yes, the salt cellars. It is a pity. You —you were proud of them?

*Persomé.* Proud of them. Why, they have been in our family for years.

*Bishop.* Yes, it is a pity. They were beautiful; but still, dear, one can eat salt out of china just as well.

*Persomé.* Yes, or meat off the floor, I suppose. Oh, it's coming to that. And as for that old wretch, Mère Gringoire, I wonder she had the audacity to send here again. The last time I saw her I gave her such a talking to that it ought to have had some effect.

*Bishop.* Yes! I offered to take her in here for a day or two, but she seemed to think it might distress you.

*Persomé.* Distress me ! ! !

*Bishop.* And the bailiff, who is a very just man,

would not wait longer for the rent, so—so—you see I *had* to pay it.

*Persomé.* *You had* to pay it. [*Gesture of comic despair.*]

*Bishop.* Yes, and you see I had no money, so I had to dispose of the salt cellars. It was fortunate I had them, wasn't it ? [*smiling*]. But I'm sorry I have grieved you.

*Persomé.* Oh, go on ! go on ! you are incorrigible. You'll sell your candlesticks next.

*Bishop* [*with real concern*]. No, no, sister, not my candlesticks.

*Persomé.* Oh ! Why not ? They would pay somebody's rent, I suppose.

*Bishop.* Ah, you are good, sister, to think of that ; but—but I don't want to sell them. You see, dear, my mother gave them to me on—on her death-bed just after you were born, and—and she asked me to keep them in remembrance of her, so I would like to keep them ; but perhaps it is a sin to set such store by them ?

*Persomé.* Brother, brother, you will break my heart [*with tears in her voice*]. There ! don't say anything more. Kiss me and give me your blessing. I am going to bed. [*They kiss.*]

[BISHOP *makes the sign of the cross and murmurs a blessing.* PERSOMÉ *locks cupboard door and goes* R.

*Persomé.* Don't sit up too long and tire your eyes.

*Bishop.* No, dear ! Good-night ! [PERSOMÉ *exits* R.

*Bishop* [*comes to table and opens a book, then looks up at the candlesticks*]. They would pay somebody's rent. It was kind of her to think of that. [*He stirs the fire, trims the lamp, arranges some books and papers, sits down, is restless, shivers slightly; clock outside strikes twelve and he settles to read. Music during this. Enter the* CONVICT *stealthily ; he has a long knife and seizes the* BISHOP *from behind.*]

*Convict.* If you call out you are a dead man !

*Bishop.* But, my friend, as you see, I am reading. Why should I call out ?  Can I help you in any way ?

*Convict* [*hoarsely*]. I want food.  I'm starving.  I haven't eaten anything for three days.  Give me food quickly, quickly, curse you.

*Bishop* [*eagerly*]. But certainly, my son, you shall have food.  I will ask my sister for the keys of the cupboard [*rising*].

*Convict.* Sit down ! ! !        [*The* BISHOP *sits smiling.* None of that, my friend !  I'm too old a bird to be caught with chaff.  You would ask your sister for the keys, would you ?  A likely story !  You would rouse the house too.  Eh ?  Ha !  ha !  A good joke truly. Come, where is the food ?  I want no keys.  I have a wolf inside me tearing at my entrails, tearing me ; quick, tell me where the food is.

*Bishop* [*aside*]. I wish Persomé would not lock the cupboard.  [*Aloud*] Come, my friend, you have nothing to fear.  My sister and I are alone here.

*Convict.* How do I know that ?

*Bishop.* Why, I have just told you.

                      [CONVICT *looks long at the* BISHOP.
*Convict.* Humph !  I'll risk it.

                      [BISHOP, *going to door* R.
But mind !  Play me false, and as sure as there are devils in Hell I'll drive my knife through your heart. I have nothing to lose.

*Bishop.* You have your soul to lose, my son ; it is of more value than my heart.  [*At door* R., *calling*] Persomé, Persomé.

   [*The* CONVICT *stands behind him with his knife ready.*

*Persomé* [*within*]. Yes, brother.

*Bishop.* Here is a poor traveller who is hungry.  If you are not undressed will you come and open the cupboard and I will give him some supper.

*Persomé* [*within*]. What, at this time of night ?  A

2

pretty business truly. Are we to have no sleep now, but to be at the beck and call of every ne'er-do-weel who happens to pass?

*Bishop.* But, Persomé, the traveller is hungry.

*Persomé.* Oh, very well, I am coming. [PERSOMÉ *enters* R., *she sees the knife in the* CONVICT'S *hand.— Frightened*] Brother, what is he doing with that knife?

*Bishop.* The knife—oh, well, you see, dear, perhaps he may have thought that I—I had *sold* ours.

[*Laughs gently.*

*Persomé.* Brother, I am frightened. He glares at us like a wild beast [*aside to him*].

*Convict.* Hurry, I tell you. Give me food or I'll stick my knife in you both and help myself.

*Bishop.* Give me the keys, Persomé [*she gives them to him*]. And now, dear, you may go to bed.

[PERSOMÉ *going. The* CONVICT *springs in front of her.*

*Convict.* Stop! Neither of you leave this room till I do.                          [*She looks at the* BISHOP.

*Bishop.* Persomé, will you favour this gentleman with your company at supper? He evidently desires it.

*Persomé.* Very well, brother.

[*She sits down at table staring at the two.*

*Bishop.* Here is some cold pie and a bottle of wine and some bread.

*Convict.* Put them on the table, and stand below it so that I can see you.

[BISHOP *does so, and opens drawer in table, taking out knife and fork, looking at the knife in* CONVICT'S *hand.*

*Convict. My* knife is sharp. [*He runs his finger along the edge and looks at them meaningly.*] And as for forks [*taking it up*], faugh! *steel* [*he throws it away*]. We don't use forks in prison.

*Persomé.* Prison?

*Convict* [*cutting off an enormous slice, which he tears*

*with his fingers like an animal. Then starts*]. What was that ? [*He looks at the door.*] Why the devil do you leave the window unshuttered and the door unbarred so that any one can come in ? [*Shutting them*].

*Bishop.* That is why they are left open.

*Convict.* Well, they are shut now !

*Bishop* [*sighs*]. For the first time in thirty years.

[CONVICT *eats voraciously and throws a bone on the floor.*

*Persomé.* Oh, my nice clean floor !

[BISHOP *picks up the bone and puts it on plate.*

*Convict.* You're not afraid of thieves ?

*Bishop.* I am sorry for them.

*Convict.* Sorry for them. Ha ! ha ! ha ! [*Drinks from bottle.*] That's a good one. Sorry for them. Ha ! ha ! ha ! [*Drinks.*] [*Suddenly*] What the devil are you ?

*Bishop.* I am a Bishop.

*Convict.* Ha ! ha ! ha ! A Bishop. Holy Virgin, a Bishop. Well, I'm damned !

*Bishop.* I hope you may escape that, my son. Persomé, you may leave us ; this gentleman will excuse you.

*Persomé.* Leave you with——

*Bishop.* Please ! My friend and I can talk more—freely then.

[*By this time, owing to his starving condition, the wine has affected him.*

*Convict.* What's that ? Leave us. Yes, yes, leave us. Good-night. I want to talk to the Bishop. The Bishop. Ha ! ha ! [*Laughs as he drinks, and coughs.*

*Bishop.* Good-night, Persomé.

[*He holds the door open and she goes out* R., *holding in her skirts as she passes the* CONVICT.

*Convict* [*chuckling to himself*]. The Bishop. Ha ! ha ! Well, I'm—— [*Suddenly very loudly*] D'you know what I am ?

*Bishop.* I think one who has suffered much.

*Convict.* Suffered? [*puzzled*] suffered? My God, yes. [*Drinks.*] But that's a long time ago. Ha! ha! That was when I was a man. Now I'm not a man; now I'm a number: number 15,729, and I've lived in Hell for ten years.

*Bishop.* Tell me about it—about Hell.

*Convict.* Why? [*Suspiciously*] Do you want to tell the police—to set them on my track?

*Bishop.* No! I will not tell the police.

*Convict* [*looks at him earnestly*]. I believe you [*scratching his head*], but damn me if I know why.

*Bishop* [*laying his hand on the* CONVICT'S *arm*]. Tell me about the time—the time before you went to—Hell.

*Convict.* It's so long ago I forget; but I had a little cottage, there were vines growing on it. [*Dreamily*] They looked pretty with the evening sun on them, and, and—there was a woman—she was [*thinking hard*]—she must have been my wife—yes. [*Suddenly and very rapidly*] Yes, I remember! She was ill, we had no food, I could get no work, it was a bad year, and my wife, my Jeanette, was ill, dying [*pause*], so I stole to buy her food. [*Long pause; the* BISHOP *gently pats his hand.*] They caught me. I pleaded to them, I told them why I stole, but they laughed at me, and I was sentenced to ten years in the prison hulks [*pause*], ten years in Hell. The night I was sentenced the gaoler told me—told me Jeanette was dead. [*Sobs with fury*] Ah, damn them, damn them. God curse them all.          [*He sinks on the table, sobbing.*

*Bishop.* Now tell me about the prison ship, about Hell.

*Convict.* Tell you about it? Look here, I was a man once. I'm a beast now, and they made me what I am. They chained me up like a wild animal, they lashed me like a hound. I fed on filth, I was covered with vermin, I slept on boards, and I complained. Then they lashed me again. For ten years, ten years.

Oh God ! They took away my name, they took away my soul, and they gave me a devil in its place; but one day they were careless, one day they forgot to chain up their wild beast, and he escaped. He was free. That was six weeks ago. I was free, free to starve.

*Bishop.* To starve ?

*Convict.* Yes, to starve. They feed you in Hell, but when you escape from it you starve. They were hunting me everywhere, and I had no passport, no name. So I stole again. I stole these rags. I stole my food daily. I slept in the woods, in barns, anywhere. I dare not ask for work, I dare not go into a town to beg, so I stole, and they have made me what I am, they have made me a thief. God curse them all.

[*Empties the bottle and throws it into the fireplace* R., *smashing it.*

*Bishop.* My son, you have suffered much, but there is hope for all.

*Convict.* Hope ! Hope ! Ha ! ha ! ha !

[*Laughs wildly.*

*Bishop.* You have walked far; you are tired. Lie down and sleep on the couch there and I will get you some coverings.

*Convict.* And if any one comes ?

*Bishop.* No one will come; but if they do, are you not my friend ?

*Convict.* Your friend ? [*puzzled.*]

*Bishop.* They will not molest the Bishop's friend.

*Convict.* The Bishop's friend.

[*Scratching his head utterly puzzled.*

*Bishop.* I will get the coverings. [*Exit* L.

*Convict* [*looks after him, scratches his head*]. The Bishop's friend ! [*He goes to fire to warm himself and notices the candlesticks. He looks round to see if he is alone, and takes them down, weighing them.*] Silver, by God, and heavy. What a prize !

[*He hears the* BISHOP *coming, and in his haste drops one candlestick on the table.*

[*Enter the* BISHOP.]

*Bishop* [*sees what is going on, but goes to the settle up* L. *with coverings*]. Ah, you are admiring my candlesticks. I am proud of them. They were a gift from my mother. A little too handsome for this poor cottage perhaps, but all I have to remind me of her. Your bed is ready. Will you lie down now ?

*Convict.* Yes, yes, I'll lie down now. [*Puzzled*] Look here, why the devil are you—ki—kind to me ? [*Suspiciously*] What do you want ? Eh ?

*Bishop.* I want you to have a good sleep, my friend.

*Convict.* I believe you want to convert me ; save my soul, don't you call it ? Well, it's no good—see ? I don't want any damned religion, and as for the Church—Bah ! I hate the Church.

*Bishop.* That is a pity, my son, as the Church does not hate you.

*Convict.* You are going to try to convert me. Oh ! Ha ! ha ! that's a good idea. Ha ! ha ! ha ! No, no, Monseigneur the Bishop. I don't want any of your Faith, Hope, and Charity—see ? So anything you do for me you're doing to the devil—understand ? [*defiantly*].

*Bishop.* One must do a great deal for the devil in order to do a little for God.

*Convict* [*angrily*]. I don't want any damned religion, I tell you.

*Bishop.* Won't you lie down now ? It is late ?

*Convict* [*grumbling*]. Well, all right ; but I won't be preached at, I—I—— [*On couch*] You're sure no one will come ?

*Bishop.* I don't think they will ; but if they do— you yourself have locked the door.

*Convict.* Humph ! I wonder if it's safe ? [*He goes to the door and tries it, then turns and sees the* BISHOP *holding the covering, annoyed*] Here ! you go to bed. I'll cover myself. [*The* BISHOP *hesitates.*] Go on, I tell you.

*Bishop.* Good-night, my son.                    [*Exit* L.

[CONVICT *waits till he is off, then tries the* BISHOP'S *door.*

*Convict.* No lock, of course.  Curse it.  [*Looks round and sees the candlesticks again.*] Humph!  I'll have another look at them.  [*He takes them up and toys with them.*] Worth hundreds, I'll warrant.  If I had these turned into money they'd start me fair.  Humph! The old boy's fond of them too, said his mother gave him them.  His mother, yes.  They didn't think of *my* mother when they sent me to Hell.  He was kind to me too—but what's a Bishop for except to be kind to you?  Here, cheer up, my hearty, you're getting soft.  God! wouldn't my chain mates laugh to see 15,729 hesitating about collaring the plunder because he felt good.  Good! Ha! ha!  Oh, my God!  Good! Ha! ha!  15,729 getting soft.  That's a good one. Ha! ha!  No, I'll take his candlesticks and go.  If I stay here he'll preach at me in the morning and I'll get soft.  Damn him and his preaching too.  Here goes!

[*He takes the candlesticks, stows them in his coat, and cautiously exits* L. C.  *As he does so the door slams.*

*Persomé* [*without*].  Who's there?  Who's there, I say?  Am I to get no sleep to-night?  Who's there, I say?  [*Enter* R. PERSOMÉ.]  I'm sure I heard the door shut.  [*Looking round*] No one here?  [*Knocks at the* BISHOP'S *door* L.  *Sees the candlesticks have gone.*] The candlesticks, the candlesticks.  They are gone. Brother, brother, come out.  Fire, murder, thieves!

[*Enter* BISHOP, L.]

*Bishop.* What is it, dear, what is it?  What is the matter?

*Persomé.* He has gone.  The man with the hungry eyes has gone, and he has taken your candlesticks.

*Bishop.* Not my candlesticks, sister, surely not

those? [*He looks and sighs.*] Ah, that is hard, very hard. I, I—— He might have left me those. They were all I had [*almost breaking down*].

*Persomé.* Well, but go and inform the police. He can't have gone far. They will soon catch him, and you'll get the candlesticks back again. You don't deserve them, though, leaving them about with a man like that in the house.

*Bishop.* You are right, Persomé. It was my fault. I led him into temptation.

*Persomé.* Oh, nonsense! led him into temptation indeed! The man is a thief, a common scoundrelly thief. I knew it the moment I saw him. Go and inform the police or I will. [*Going ; but he stops her.*

*Bishop.* And have him sent back to prison, [*very softly*] sent back to Hell! No, Persomé. It is a just punishment for me ; I set too great store by them. It was a sin. My punishment is just; but, oh God, it is hard, it is very hard. [*He buries his head in his hands.*

*Persomé.* No, brother, you are wrong. If you won't tell the police, I will. I will not stand by and see you robbed. I know you are my brother and my Bishop, and the best man in all France ; but you are a fool, I tell you, a child, and I will not have your goodness abused. I shall go and inform the police. [*Going.*

*Bishop.* Stop, Persomé. The candlesticks were mine; they are *his* now. It is better so. He has more need of them than I. My mother would have wished it so had she been here.

*Persomé.* But—— [*Great knocking without.*

*Sergeant* [*without*]. Monseigneur, Monseigneur, we have something for you. May we enter ?

*Bishop.* Enter, my son.

[*Enter* SERGEANT *and three* GENDARMES *with* CONVICT *bound. The* SERGEANT *carries the candlesticks.*]

*Persomé.* Ah, so they have caught you, villain, have they ?

*Sergeant.* Yes, madam, we found this scoundrel slinking along the road, and as he wouldn't give any account of himself we arrested him on suspicion. Holy Virgin, isn't he strong and didn't he struggle ? While we were securing him these candlesticks fell out of his pockets.

[PERSOME *seizes them, goes to table, and brushes them with her apron lovingly.*

I remembered the candlesticks of Monseigneur the Bishop, so we brought him here that you might identify them, and then we'll lock him up.

[*The* BISHOP *and the* CONVICT *have been looking at each other—the* CONVICT *with dogged defiance.*

*Bishop.* But—but I don't understand ; this gentleman is my very good friend.

*Sergeant.* Your *friend*, Monseigneur ! ! Holy Virgin ! Well ! ! !

*Bishop.* Yes, my friend. He did me the honour to sup with me to-night, and I—I have given him the candlesticks.

*Sergeant* [*incredulously*]. You gave *him*—him your candlesticks ? Holy Virgin !

*Bishop* [*severely*]. Remember, my son, that she is holy.

*Sergeant* [*saluting*]. Pardon, Monseigneur.

*Bishop.* And now I think you may let your prisoner go.

*Sergeant.* But he won't show me his papers ; he won't tell me who he is.

*Bishop.* I have told you he is my friend.

*Sergeant.* Yes, that's all very well, but——

*Bishop.* He is your Bishop's friend ; surely that is enough.

*Sergeant.* Well, but——

*Bishop.* Surely ?  [*A pause.*

[*The* SERGEANT *and the* BISHOP *look at each other.*

*Sergeant.* I—I—Humph ! [*To his men*] Loose the prisoner. [*They do so.*] Right about turn, quick march !

[*Exit* SERGEANT *and* GENDARMES. *A long pause.*

*Convict* [*very slowly, as if in a dream*]. You told

them you had given me the candlesticks—given me
them. By God!

*Persomé* [*shaking her fist at him and hugging the
candlesticks to her breast*]. Oh, you scoundrel, you pitiful scoundrel. You come here, and are fed, and
warmed, and—and you thieve; steal from your bene-
factor. Oh, you blackguard.

*Bishop*. Persomé, you are overwrought. Go to your
room.

*Persomé*. What, and leave you with him to be
cheated again, perhaps murdered? No, I will not.

*Bishop* [*with slight severity*]. Persomé, leave us. I
wish it.

[*She looks hard at him, then turns towards her door.*

*Persomé*. Well, if I must go, at least I'll take the
candlesticks with me.

*Bishop* [*more severely*]. Persomé, place the candlesticks on that table and leave us.

*Persomé* [*defiantly*]. I will not!

*Bishop* [*loudly and with great severity*]. I, your
Bishop, command it.

[PERSOMÉ *does so with great reluctance and exits* R.

*Convict* [*shamefacedly*]. Monseigneur, I'm glad I
didn't get away with them; curse me, I am. I'm glad.

*Bishop*. Now won't you sleep here? See, your bed
is ready.

*Convict*. No! [*looking at the candlesticks*]. No! no!
I daren't, I daren't. Besides, I must go on, I must get
to Paris; it is big, and I—I can be lost there. They
won't find me there. And I must travel at night. Do
you understand?

*Bishop*. I see—you must travel by night.

*Convict*. I—I—didn't believe there was any good
in the world; one doesn't when one has been in Hell;
but somehow I—I—know you're good, and—and it's a
queer thing to ask, but—but could you, would you bless
me before I go? I—I think it would help me. I——

[*Hangs his head very shamefacedly.*

[BISHOP *makes sign of the cross and murmurs blessing.*

*Convict* [*tries to speak, but a sob almost chokes him*]. Good-night.                    [*He hurries towards the door.*

*Bishop.* Stay, my son, you have forgotten your property [*giving him the candlesticks*].

*Convict.* You mean me—you want me to take them ?

*Bishop.* Please ; they may help you.

[*The* CONVICT *takes the candlesticks in absolute amazement.*

*Bishop.* And, my son, there is a path through the woods at the back of this cottage which leads to Paris ; it is a very lonely path, and I have noticed that my good friends the gendarmes do not like lonely paths at night. It is curious.

*Convict.* Ah, thanks, thanks, Monseigneur. I—I— [*He sobs.*] Ah! I'm a fool, a child to cry, but somehow you have made me feel that—that it is just as if something had come into me—as if I were a man again and not a wild beast.

[*The door at back is open and the* CONVICT *is standing in it.*

*Bishop* [*putting his hand on his shoulder*]. Always remember, my son, that this poor body is the Temple of the Living God.

*Convict* [*with great awe*]. The Temple of the Living God.  I'll remember.                    [*Exit* L. C.

[*The* BISHOP *closes the door and goes quietly to the Priedieu in the window* R., *he sinks on his knees, and bows his head in prayer.*


SLOW  CURTAIN

# THE PHILOSOPHER OF BUTTER-BIGGINS

## By Harold Chapin

Produced for the first time on December 14, 1915, at THE HAROLD CHAPIN MEMORIAL PERFORMANCE, with the following cast:

| | | |
|---|---|---|
| DAVID | . . . . . | Mr. Campbell Gullan. |
| LIZZIE | . . . . . | Miss Hilda Trevelyan. |
| JOHN | . . . . . | Mr. Allan Jeayes. |
| WEE ALEXANDER | . . | Master Harold Valetta Chapin. |

Afterwards by the Stage Society, on December 17, 1917, with the following cast:

| | | |
|---|---|---|
| DAVID | . . . . . | Mr. Campbell Gullan. |
| LIZZIE | . . . . . | Miss Norah Balfour. |
| JOHN | . . . . . | Mr. George Howard |
| WEE ALEXANDER | . . | Master Harold Valetta Chapin. |

## CHARACTERS

DAVID PIRNIE.
LIZZIE, *his daughter*.
JOHN BELL, *his son-in-law*.
ALEXANDER, *John's little son*.

# THE PHILOSOPHER OF BUTTER-BIGGINS

[JOHN BELL'S *house in the tenement at Butterbiggins consists of the very usual " two rooms, kitchen and bath," a concealed bed in the parlour and another in the kitchen enabling him to house his family—consisting of himself, his wife, his little son, and his aged father-in-law— therein. The kitchen and living-room is a good-sized square room. The right wall (our* R. *as we look at it) is occupied by a huge built-in dresser, sink, and coal-bunker ; the* L. *wall by a high-mantelled, ovened and boilered fireplace, the recess on either side of which contains a low, painted cupboard. Over the far cupboard hangs a picture of a ship, but over the near one is a small, square window. The far wall has two large doors in it, that on the right leading to the lobby, and that on the left appertaining to the old father-in-law's concealed bed.*

*The walls are distempered a brickish red. The ceiling once was white. The floor is covered with bright linoleum and a couple of rag rugs—one before the fire—a large one —and one smaller one before the door of the concealed bed.*

*A deal table is just to* R. *of centre, a long flexible gas-bracket depending from the ceiling above it. Another many-jointed gas-bracket projects from the middle of the high mantelpiece, its flame turned down towards the stove. There are wooden chairs at the table, above, below, and to* L. *of it—the latter chair being in the centre. A high-backed easy-chair is above the fire, a kitchen elbow-chair below it.*

*The kitchen is very tidy. A newspaper newly fallen*

*on the rug before the fire and another—an evening one—
spread flat on the table are (besides a child's mug and
plate also on the table) the only things not stowed in their
prescribed places. It is evening—the light beyond the
little square window being the grey dimness of a long
Northern twilight which slowly deepens during the play.
When the curtain rises it is still light enough in the room
for a man to read if the print be not too faint and his eyes
good. The warm light of the fire leaps and flickers
through the grey, showing up with exceptional clearness
the deep-lined face of old DAVID PIRNIE, who is discovered half-risen from his arm-chair, above the fire standing
on the hearth-rug, his body bent and his hand on the chair
arm. He is a little, feeble old man with a well-shaped
head and weather-beaten face, set off by a grizzled beard
and whiskers wiry and vigorous in curious contrast to the
wreath of snowy hair that encircles his head. His upper
lip is shaven. He wears an old suit—the waistcoat of
which, being unbuttoned, shows an old flannel shirt. His
slippers are low at the heel and his socks loose at the
ankles.*

*The old man's eyes are fixed appealingly on those of his
daughter, who stands in the half-open door, her grasp on
the handle, meeting his look squarely—a straight-browed,
black-haired, determined young woman of six- or seven-
and-twenty. Her husband, JOHN, seated at the table in
his shirt-sleeves with his head in his hands, reads hard at
the paper and tries to look unconcerned.*]

*David.* Aw—but Lizzie !

*Lizzie* [*with splendid firmness*]. It's nae use, faither.
I'm no' gaein' to gie in to the wean. Ye've been
tellin' yer stories to him nicht after nicht for dear
knows how long and he's gettin' to expect them.

*David.* Why should he no' expect them ?

*Lizzie.* It disna do for weans to count on things so.
He's layin' up a sad disappointment for himself yin o'
these days.

*David.* He's gettin' a sad disappointment the noo. Och, come on, Lizzie ! I'm no' gaein' to die just yet, an' ye can break him off gradually when I begin to look like it.

*Lizzie.* Wha's talkin' of yer diein', faither ?

*David.* Ye were speakin' o' the disappointment he was layin' up for himself if he got to count on me.

*Lizzie.* I wasna thinkin' o' yer diein', faither—only —it's no' guid for a bairn——

*David.* Where's the harm in my giein' him a bit story before he gangs tae his bed ?

*Lizzie.* I'm no' sayin' there's ony harm in it this yinst, faither ; but it's no' richt to gae on nicht after nicht wi' never a break——

*David.* Whit wey is it no' richt if there's nae harm in it ?

*Lizzie.* It's giein' in to the wean.

*David.* Whit wey should ye no' gie in to him if there's nae harm in it ?

*Lizzie* [*keeping her patience with difficulty*]. Because it gets him into the habit.

*David.* But why should he no' get into the habit if there's nae harm in it ?

[JOHN, *at the table, chuckles.* LIZZIE *gives him a look, but he meets it not.*

*Lizzie.* Really, faither, ye micht be a wean yersel', ye're that persistent.

*David.* No, Lizzie, I'm no' persistent. I'm reasoning wi' ye. Ye said there was nae harm in my telling him a wee bit story, an' now ye say I'm not to because it'll get him into the habit, an' what I'm askin' ye is, where's the harm o' his gettin' into the habit if there's nae harm in it ?

*Lizzie.* Oh, aye ; ye can be gey clever, twisting the words in my mouth, faither ; but richt's richt, and wrang's wrang for a' yer cleverness.

*David* [*earnestly*]. I'm no' bein' clever ava', Lizzie— no' the noo—I'm just trying to make ye see that if ye

3

admit there's nae harm in a thing ye canna say there's ony harm in it an'—[*pathetically*]—I'm wantin' to tell wee Alexander a bit story before he gangs to his bed.

*John* [*aside to her*]. Och, wumman——

*Lizzie.* T'ts, John, ye'd gie in tae onybody if they were just persistent enough.

*John.* He's an auld man.

*Lizzie* [*really exasperated*]. I ken fine he's an auld man, John, and ye're a young yin, an' Alexander's gaein' to be anither, an' I'm a lone wumman among the lot o' ye, but I'm no' gaein' to gie in to——

*John* [*bringing a fresh mind to bear upon the argument*]. Efter a', Lizzie, there's nae harm——

*Lizzie* [*almost with a scream of anger*]. Och, now you've stairted, have you? Harm! Harm! Harm! You're talking about *harm* and I'm talking about richt and wrang. You'd see your son grow up a drunken keelie an' mebbe a thief an' a murderer so long as you could say there was nae harm in it.

*John* [*expostulating with some cause*]. But I couldna say there was nae harm in that, Lizzie, an' I wudna. Only when there's nae harm——

*Lizzie.* Och!! [*Exits, calling off to the cause of the trouble.*] Are ye in yer bed yet, Alexander? [*Shuts door with a click.*]

*David* [*standing on hearthrug and shaking his head more in sorrow than in anger*]. She's no' reasonable, ye ken, John; she disna argue fair. I'm no' complainin' o' her mither; but it's a wee bit hard that the only twa women I've known well enough to be really chatty an' argumentative with, should have been just like that. An' me that fond o' women's society! [*He lowers himself into his chair.*]

*John.* They're all like it.

*David* [*judiciously*]. I wudna go sae far as to say that, John. Ye see, I've only kent they twa to study carefully—an' it's no' fair to judge the whole sex by just the twa examples as it were [*running on*]—but it's gey hard, an' I was wantin' to tell wee Alexander a special fine story the nicht. [*Removes glasses and blinks his eyes.*] Aweel !

*John* [*comforting*]. Mebbe the morn——

*David.* If it's no' richt the nicht, it'll no' be richt the morn's nicht.

*John.* Ye canna say that, faither. It wasna wrang last nicht.

*David* [*bitterly*]. Mebbe it was, an' Lizzie hadna foun' it out.

*John.* Aw noo, faither, dinna get saurcastic !

*David* [*between anger and tears weakly*]. I canna help it. I'm black affronted. I was wantin' to tell wee Alexander a special fine story the nicht, an' now here's Lizzie wi' her richt's richt an' wrang's wrang. Och ! there's nae reason in the women !

*John.* We hae to gie in to them, though.

*David.* Aye ! That's why.

> [*There is a pause. The old man picks up his paper again and settles his glasses on his nose.* JOHN *rises and, with a spill from the mantelpiece, lights the gas there, which he then bends to throw the light to the old man's advantage.*]

*David.* Thank ye, John. Do ye hear him ?

*John* [*erect on hearthrug*]. Who ?

*David.* Wee Alexander.

*John.* No.

*David.* Greetin' his heart out.

*John.* Och, he's no' greetin'. Lizzie's wi' him.

*David.* I ken fine Lizzie's wi' him, but he's greetin' for a' that. He was wantin' to hear yon story o' the kelpies up at Crosshill wi' the tram—[*breaking his mood impatiently*]—Och !

*John* [*crossing to table and lighting up there*]. It's gettin' dark gey early. We'll shin be haein' tea by the gas.

*David* [*rustling his paper*]. Aye—— [*Suddenly*] There never was a female philosopher, ye ken, John.

*John.* Was there no' ?

*David.* No. [*Angrily in a gust.*] An' there never will be ! [*Then more calmly.*] An' yet there's an awful lot o' philosophy about women, John.

*John.* Aye ?

*David.* O aye. They're that unreasonable, an' yet ye canna reason them down, an' they're that weak, an' yet ye canna make them gie in to ye. Of course ye'll say ye canna reason doon a stane or make a clod o' earth gie in tae ye.

*John.* Will I ?

*David.* Aye. An' ye'll be richt. But then I'll tell ye a stane willna answer ye back, an' a clod o' earth willna try to withstand ye, so how can ye argue them down ?

*John* [*convinced*]. Ye canna.

*David.* Richt ! Ye canna ! But a wumman *will* answer ye back, an' she *will* stand against ye, an' *yet* ye canna argue her down, though ye have strength an' reason on your side, an' she's talkin' naething but blethers about richt's richt and wrang's wrang, an' sending a poor bairn off t' his bed i' the yin room, an' leavin' her auld faither all alone by the fire in the ither, an'—ye ken—philosophy—— [*He ceases to speak, and wipes his glasses again.*]

> [JOHN, *intensely troubled, tiptoes up to the door and opens it a foot. The wails of* ALEXANDER *can be heard muffled by a further door.* JOHN *calls off.*]

*John.* Lizzie.

> [LIZZIE *immediately comes into sight outside the door with a " shsh."*]

*John.* Yer faither's greetin' !

*Lizzie* [*with a touch of exasperation*]. Och, I'm no' heedin'. There's anither wean in there greetin' too, an' I'm no' heedin' him neither, and he's greetin' twicet as loud as the auld yin.

*John* [*shocked*]. Ye're heartless, wumman.

*Lizzie* [*with patience*]. No, I'm no heartless, John, but there's too much heart in this family, an' somebody's got to use their heid.

[DAVID *cranes round the side of his chair to catch what they are saying. She stops and comes to him kindly, but with womanly firmness.*

*Lizzie.* I'm vexed ye should be disappointed, faither, but ye see, don't ye——

[*A singularly piercing wail from* ALEXANDER *goes up.* LIZZIE *rushes to silence him.*

*Lizzie.* Mercy ! The neighbours will think we're murderin' him. [*The door closes behind her.*

*David* [*nodding for a space as he revolves the woman's attitude*]. Ye hear that, John ?

*John.* Whit ?

*David* [*with quiet irony*]. She's vexed I should be disappointed. The wumman thinks she's richt ! Wummen aye think they're richt—mebbe it's that that mak's them that obstinate. [*With a ghost of a twinkle.*] She's feart o' the neighbours, though.

*John* [*stolidly*]. A' women are feart o' the neighbours.

*David* [*reverting*]. Puir wee man. I telt ye he was greetin', John. He's fine an' disappointed. [*Pondering.*] D'ye ken what I'm thinkin', John ?

*John.* Whit ?

*David.* I'm thinkin' he's ower young to get his ain wey, an' I'm ower auld, an' it's a fine thocht !

*John.* Aye ?

*David.* Aye. I never thocht of it before, but that's what it is. He's no' come to it yet, an' I'm past it. [*Suddenly.*] What's the most important thing in life, John ?

[JOHN *opens his mouth and shuts it again unused.*

*David.* Ye ken perfectly well. What is it ye're wantin' a' the time ?

*John.* Different things.

*David* [*satisfied*]. Aye—different things ! But ye want them a', do ye no' ?

*John.* Aye.

*David.* If ye had yer ain wey ye'd hae them, eh ?

*John.* I wud that.

*David* [*triumphant*]. Then is that no' what ye want :
yer ain wey ?

*John* [*enlightened*]. Losh !

*David* [*warming to it*]. That's what life is, John—
gettin' yer ain wey. First ye're born, an' ye canna
dae anything but cry ; but God's given yer mither ears,
an' ye get yer wey by just cryin' for it. [*Hastily
anticipating criticism.*] I ken that's no' exactly in
keeping wi' what I've been sayin' aboot Alexander—
but a new-born bairnie's an awfu' delicate thing, an'
the Lord gets it past its infancy by a dispensation o'
Providence very unsettling to oor poor human under-
standings. Ye'll notice the weans cease getting their
wey by juist greetin' for it as shin as they're auld
enough to seek it otherwise.

*John*. The habit hangs on to them whiles.

*David* [*with a twinkle*]. It does that. An' mebbe
if God's given yer neighbours ears an' ye live close by
ye'll get yer wey by a dispensation o' Providence a
while longer. But there's things ye'll hae to do for
yourself gin ye want to—an' ye will—ye'll want to
hold up yer hand, an' ye *will* hold up yer hand, an'
ye'll want to stand up an' walk, an' ye *will* stand up
an' walk, an' ye'll want to dae as ye please, an' ye *will*
dae as ye please, an' then ye are practised an' learnt
in the art of getting yer ain wey—an' ye're a man !

*John*. Man, faither, ye're wonderful !

*David* [*complacently*]. I'm a philosopher, John. But
it goes on mebbe.

*John*. Aye ?

*David*. Aye, mebbe ye think ye'd like to make ither
folk mind ye an' yer wey an' ye try, an' if it comes off
ye're a big man an' mebbe the master o' a vessel wi'
three men and a boy under ye as I was, John.
[*Dropping into the minor.*] An' then ye come doon hill.

*John* [*apprehensively*]. Doon the hill ?

*David*. Aye—doon to mebbe wantin' to tell a wean
a bit story before he gangs tae his bed, an' ye canna

dae even that. An' then a while more an' ye want
to get to yer feet an' ye canna, an' a while more an'
ye want to lift up yer hand an' ye canna . . . an' in
a while more ye're just forgotten an' done wi'.

*John.* Aw, faither !

*David.* Dinna look sae troubled, John. I'm no
afraid to die when my time comes. It's these hints
that I'm done wi' before I'm dead that I dinna like.

*John.* Whatna hints ?

*David.* Well—Lizzie an' her richt's richt an' wrang's
wrang when I think o' telling wee Alexander a wee bit
story before he gangs tae his bed.

*John* [*gently*]. Ye are a wee thing persistent, faither.

*David.* No, I'm no' persistent, John. I've gied in.
I'm a philosopher, John, an' a philosopher kens when
he's done wi'.

*John.* Aw, faither.

*David* [*getting lower and lower*]. It's gey interesting, philosophy, John, an' the only philosophy worth
thinkin' about is the philosophy of growin' auld—
because that's what we're a' doing, a' living things.
There's nae philosophy in a stane, John, he's juist a
stane, an' in a hun'red years he'll be juist a stane still
—unless he's broken up, an' then he'll be juist not a
stane, but he'll no' ken what's happened to him because he didn't break up gradual an' first lose his boat
an' then his hoose, an' then hae his wee grandson
taken away when he was for tellin' him a bit story
before he gangs tae his bed. . . . It's yon losing yer
grip bit by bit an' kennin that ye're losing it that
makes a philosopher, John.

*John.* If I kent what ye meant by philosophy,
faither, I'd be better able to follow ye.

[LIZZIE *enters quietly and closes door after her.*

*John.* Is he asleep ?

*Lizzie.* No, he's no' asleep, but I've shut both doors,
an' the neighbours canna hear him.

*John.* Aw, Lizzie——

*Lizzie* [*sharply*.] John——

*David*. Whit was I tellin' ye, John, about weans gettin' their ain wey if the neighbours had ears an' they lived close ?   Was I no' richt ?

*Lizzie* [*answering for John with some acerbity*]. Aye, ye were richt, faither, nae doot, but we dinna live that close here, an' the neighbours canna hear him at the back o' the hoose.

*David*. Mebbe that's why ye changed Alexander into the parlour an' gied me the bed in here when it began to get cauld.

*Lizzie* [*hurt*]. Aw no, faither, I brought ye in here to be warmer.

*David* [*placably*]. I believe ye, wumman—[*with a faint twinkle again*]—but it's turned oot luckily, has it no' ?

> [DAVID *waits for a reply, but gets none.* LIZZIE
> *fetches needlework from dresser drawer and sits
> above table.* DAVID'S *face and voice take on a
> more thoughtful tone.*

*David* [*musing*]. Puir wee man.  If he was in here you'd no' be letting him greet his heart oot where onybody could hear him.   Wud ye ?

*Lizzie* [*calmly*]. Mebbe I'd no'.

*John*. Ye ken fine ye'd no', wumman.

*Lizzie*. John, thread my needle, and dinna take faither's part against me.

*John* [*surprised*]. I'm no'.

*Lizzie*. No, I ken ye're no' meaning to, but you men are that thrang——

> [*She is interrupted by a loud squall from* DAVID,
> *which he maintains, eyes shut, chair arms
> gripped, and mouth open, for nearly half a
> minute before he cuts it off abruptly and looks at
> the startled couple at the table.*

*Lizzie*. Mercy, faither, whit's wrang wi' ye ?

*David* [*collectedly*]. There's naething wrang wi' me, Lizzie, except that I'm wantin' to tell wee Alexander a bit story——

*Lizzie* [*firmly, but very kindly*]. But ye're no' goin'
to——

[*She breaks off in alarm as her father opens his
mouth preparatory to another yell, which, however, he postpones to speak to* JOHN.

*David.* Ye mind whit I was saying about the dispensation o' Providence to help weans till they could
try for theirsels, John ?

*John.* Aye.

*David.* Did it no' occur to ye, then, that there ought
to be some sort of dispensation to look after the auld
yins who were past it ?

*John.* No.

*David.* Aweel—it didna occur to me at the time.

[*And he lets off another prolonged wail.*

*Lizzie* [*going to him*]. Faither ! The neighbours 'll
hear ye ! !

*David* [*desisting as before*]. I ken it fine. *I'm* no'
at the back of the hoose. [*Shorter wail.*

*Lizzie* [*almost in tears*]. They'll be coming to ask.

*David.* Let them. They'll no' ask *me*. [*Squall.*

*Lizzie.* Faither—ye're no behaving well. John——

*John.* Aye ?

*Lizzie* (*helplessly*). Naething—— Faither, stop it.
They'll think ye clean daft.

*David* [*ceasing to howl, and speaking with gravity*]. I
ken it fine, Lizzie ; an' it's no' easy for a man who has
been respeckit an' lookit up to a' his life to be thought
daft at eighty-three, but the most important thing in
life is to get yer ain wey. [*Resumes wailing.*

*Lizzie* [*puzzled, to John*]. Whit's that ?

*John.* It's his philosophy that he was talking aboot.

*David* [*firmly*]. An' I'm gaein' to tell wee Alexander
yon story tho' they think me daft for it.

*Lizzie.* But it's no' for his ain guid, faither. I've
telt ye so, but ye wudna listen.

*David.* *I* wudna listen, wumman ! It was you
wudna listen to me when I axed ye whit harm.

[*Checking himself.*] No! I'm no' gaein' to hae that ower again. I've gien up arguin' wi' women. I'm juist gaein' tae greet loud an' sair till wee Alexander's brought in here to hae his bit story, an' if the neighbours——                                   [*Loud squall*

Lizzie [*aside to John*]. He's fair daft!

John [*aghast*]. Ye'd no' send him to——

Lizzie [*reproachfully*]. John!
                                   [*A louder squall from the old man.*

Lizzie [*beseechingly*]. Oh, faither——
                                   [*A still louder one.*

Lizzie [*beating her hands together distractedly*]. He'll be—— Will—— He'll—— Och!!! [*Resigned and beaten.*] John, go and bring wee Alexander in here.

[JOHN *is off like a shot. The opening of the door of the other room can be told by the burst of* ALEXANDER'S *voice. The old man's wails have stopped the second his daughter capitulated.* JOHN *returns with* ALEXANDER *and bears him to his grandfather's waiting knee. The boy's tears and howls have ceased, and he is smiling triumphantly. He is, of course, in his nightshirt and a blanket which Grandpa wraps round him, turning towards the fire.*

Lizzie [*looking on with many nods of the head and smacks of the lips*]. There you are! That's the kind o' boy he is. Greet his heart oot for a thing an' stop the moment he gets it.

David. Dae ye expect him to gae on after he's got it? Ah, but Alexander, ye didna get it yer lane this time; it took the twa o' us. An' hard work it was for the auld yin! Man [*playing hoarse*], I doot if I've enough voice left for a—— [*Bursting out very loud and making the boy laugh.*] Aweel! Whit's it gaein' to be—eh?

**CURTAIN**

# THE REHEARSAL

## By Maurice Baring

# CHARACTERS

Mr. William Shakespeare.
*The Producer.*
*The Stage Manager.*

Mr. Burbage (*Macbeth*).
Mr. Hughes (*Lady Macbeth*).
Mr. Kydd (*Banquo*).
Mr. Foote (*Macduff*).
Mr. Thomas (*The Doctor*).
Mr. Lyle (*First Witch*).
*Second Witch.*
*Third Witch.*

# THE REHEARSAL

SCENE.—*The Globe Theatre, 1606. On the stage the* AUTHOR, *the* PRODUCER, *and the* STAGE MANAGER *are standing. A rehearsal of "Macbeth" is about to begin. Waiting in the wings are the actors who are playing the* WITCHES, BANQUO, MACDUFF, *etc. They are all men.*

*The Stage Manager.* We'd better begin with the last act.

*The Producer.* I think we'll begin with the first act. We've never done it all through yet.

*The Stage Manager.* Mr. Colman isn't here. It's no good doing the first act without Duncan.

*The Producer.* Where is Mr. Colman? Did you let him know about rehearsal?

*The Stage Manager.* I sent a messenger to his house in Gray's Inn.

*The First Witch.* Mr. Colman is playing Psyche in a masque at Kenilworth. He won't be back until the day after to-morrow.

*The Producer.* That settles it. We'll begin with the fifth act.

*The First Witch.* Then I suppose I can go.

*The Second Witch.* ⎱ And I suppose we needn't
*The Third Witch.* ⎰ wait.

*The Stage Manager.* Certainly not. We're going on to the fourth act as soon as we've done the fifth.

*Banquo.* But I suppose you don't want me.

*The Stage Manager.* And what about your ghost entrance in Act IV.? We must get the business right this time ; besides, we'll do the second act if we've time.  Now, Act V., Mr. Thomas and Mr. Bowles, please.

*The First Witch.* Mr. Bowles can't come to-day. He told me to tell you.  He's having a tooth pulled out.

*The Stage Manager.* Then will you read the waiting gentlewoman's part, Mr. Lyle.  You can take this scrip.                    [*The* FIRST WITCH *takes the scrip.* Where is Mr. Thomas ?

*The First Witch.* He said he was coming.

*The Stage Manager.* We can't wait.  I'll read his part.  We'll leave out the beginning and just give Mr. Hughes his cue.

*The First Witch* [*reading*]. " Having no witness to confirm my speech."

*The Stage Manager.* Mr. Hughes.

*The First Witch.* He was here a moment ago.

*The Stage Manager* [*louder*]. Mr. Hughes.

[*Enter* LADY MACBETH (MR. HUGHES, *a young man about* 24).]

*Lady Macbeth.* Sorry.

[*He comes on down some steps* L. C.]

*The Producer.* That will never do, Mr. Hughes ; there's no necessity to sway as if you were intoxicated, and you mustn't look at your feet.

*Lady Macbeth.* It's the steps.  They're so rickety.

*The Producer.* We'll begin again from " speech."

[LADY MACBETH *comes on again.  He looks straight in front of him and falls heavily on to the ground.* I said those steps were to be mended yesterday.

[*The* FIRST WITCH *is convulsed with laughter.*

*Lady Macbeth.* There's nothing to laugh at.

*The Producer.* Are you hurt, Mr. Hughes ?

*Lady Macbeth.* Not much.

[*The steps are replaced by two supers.*

*The Producer.* Now from " speech."

[MR. HUGHES *comes on again.*

*The Producer.* You must not hold the taper upside down.

*Lady Macbeth.* How can I rub my hands and hold a taper too ? What's the use of the taper ?

*The Producer.* You can rub the back of your hand. You needn't wash your hands in the air. That's better.

*Gentlewoman.* " Neither to you nor any one ; having no witness to confirm my speech. Lo you, here she comes ! "

[*Enter* LADY MACBETH.]

*Gentlewoman.* " This is her very guise ; and, upon my life, fast asleep. Observe her ! stand close."

*The Doctor.* " How came she by that light ? "

*Gentlewoman.* " Why, it stood by her : she has light by her continually ; 'tis her command."

*The Doctor.* " You see, her eyes are open.'

*Gentlewoman.* " Ay, but their sense is shut."

*The Doctor.* " What is it she does now ? Look, how she rubs her hands."

*Gentlewoman.* " It is an accustomed action with her to seem thus washing her hands : I have known her continue in this a quarter of an hour."

[*Enter the* DOCTOR (MR. THOMAS). *He waits* R.]

*Lady Macbeth.* " Here's a damned spot."

*The Stage Manager.* No, no, Mr. Hughes, " Yet here's a spot."

*The Producer.* Begin again from " hands."

*Gentlewoman.* " It is an accustomed action with her to seem thus washing her hands. I've known her to continue in this three-quarters of an hour."

*Lady Macbeth.* " Yet here's a damned spot."

*The Stage Manager.* It's not " damned " at all. That comes later.

*Lady Macbeth.* It's catchy. Couldn't I say "mark" instead of "spot" in the first line?

*The Doctor* [*coming forward*]. That would entirely spoil the effect of my "Hark!" You see "mark" rhymes with "Hark." It's impossible.

*The Producer.* Oh! It's you, Mr. Thomas. Will you go straight on. We'll do the whole scene over presently. Now from "hour."

*Lady Macbeth.* "Yes, here's a spot."

*The Stage Manager.* It's not "Yes," but "Yet," Mr. Hughes.

*Lady Macbeth.* "Yet here's a spot."

*The Doctor* [*at the top of his voice*]. "Hark!"

*The Producer.* Not so loud, Mr. Thomas, that would wake her up.

*The Doctor* [*in a high falsetto*]. "Har-r-rk! She spe-e-e-aks. I will . . . set . . . down."

*The Producer.* You needn't bleat that "speaks," Mr. Thomas, and the second part of that line is cut.

*The Doctor.* It's not cut in my part. "Hark, she speaks."

*Lady Macbeth.* "Yet here's a spot."

*The Stage Manager.* No, Mr. Hughes; "out, damned spot."

*Lady Macbeth.* Sorry.

*The Producer.* We must get that right. Now from "hour."

*Lady Macbeth.* "Yet here's a spot."

*The Doctor.* "Hark! she speaks."

*Lady Macbeth.* "Get out, damned spot! Get out, I say! One, two, three, four: why there's plenty of time to do't. Oh! Hell! Fie, fie, my Lord! a soldier and a beard! What have we got to fear when none can call our murky power to swift account withal? You'd never have thought the old man had so much blood in him!"

*The Author.* I don't think you've got those lines quite right yet, Mr. Hughes.

*Lady Macbeth.* What's wrong ?

*The Stage Manager.* There's no " get." It's " one ; two " : and not " one, two, three, four." Then it's " Hell is murky." And there's no " plenty." And it's " a soldier and *afeared,*" and not " a soldier and a *beard.*"

*The Author.* And after that you made two lines into rhymed verse.

*Mr. Hughes.* Yes, I know I did. I thought it wanted it.

*The Producer.* Please try to speak your lines as they are written, Mr. Hughes.

[*Enter* MR. BURBAGE, *who plays* MACBETH.]

*Mr. Burbage.* That scene doesn't go. Now don't you think Macbeth had better walk in his sleep instead of Lady Macbeth ?

*The Stage Manager.* That's an idea.

*The Producer.* I think the whole scene might be cut. It's quite unnecessary.

*Lady Macbeth.* Then I shan't come on in the whole of the fifth act. If that scene's cut I shan't play at all.

*The Stage Manager.* We're thinking of transferring the scene to Macbeth. [*To the* AUTHOR] It wouldn't need much altering. Would you mind re-writing that scene, Mr. Shakespeare ? It wouldn't want much alteration. You'd have to change that line about Arabia. Instead of " this little hand," you might say : " All the perfumes of Arabia will not sweeten this horny hand." I'm not sure it isn't more effective.

*The Author.* I'm afraid it might get a laugh.

*Mr. Burbage.* Not if I play it.

*The Author.* I think it's more likely that Lady Macbeth would walk in her sleep, but——

*Mr. Burbage.* That doesn't signify. I can make a great hit in that scene.

*Lady Macbeth.* If you take that scene from me, I shan't play Juliet to-night.

*The Stage Manager* [*aside to* PRODUCER]. We can't possibly get another Juliet.

*The Producer.* On the whole, I think we must leave the scene as it is.

*Mr. Burbage.* I've got nothing to do in the last act. What's the use of my coming to rehearsal when there's nothing for me to rehearse ?

*The Producer.* Very well, Mr. Burbage. We'll go on to the Third Scene at once. We'll go through your scene again later, Mr. Hughes.

*Mr. Burbage.* Before we do this scene there's a point I wish to settle. In Scene V., when Seyton tells me the Queen's dead, I say : " She should have died hereafter ; there would have been a time for such a word " ; and then the messenger enters. I should like a soliloquy here, about twenty or thirty lines, if possible in rhyme, in any case ending with a tag. I should like it to be about Lady Macbeth. Macbeth might have something touching to say about their happy domestic life, and the early days of their marriage. He might refer to their courtship. I must have something to make Macbeth sympathetic, otherwise the public won't stand it. He might say his better-half had left him, and then he might refer to her beauty. The speech might begin :

> O dearest chuck, it is unkind indeed
> To leave me in the midst of my sore need.

Or something of the kind. In any case it ought to rhyme. Could I have that written at once, and then we could rehearse it ?

*The Producer.* Certainly, certainly, Mr. Burbage. Will you write it yourself, Mr. Shakespeare, or shall we get some one else to do it ?

*The Author.* I'll do it myself if some one will read my part.

*The Producer.* Let me see; I forget what is your part.

*The Stage Manager.* Mr. Shakespeare is playing Seyton. [*Aside*] We cast him for Duncan, but he wasn't up to it.

*The Producer.* Mr. Kydd, will you read Mr. Shakespeare's part?

*Banquo.* Certainly.

*The Producer.* Please let us have that speech, Mr. Shakespeare, as quickly as possible. [*Aside*] Don't make it too long. Ten lines at the most.

*The Author* [*aside*]. Is it absolutely necessary that it should rhyme?

*The Producer* [*aside*]. No, of course not; that's Burbage's fad.    [*Exit the* AUTHOR *into the wings.*

*Mr. Burbage.* I should like to go through the fight first.

*The Producer.* Very well, Mr. Burbage.

*The Stage Manager.* Macduff—Mr. Foote—

*Macduff.* I'm here.

*Mr. Burbage.* I'll give you the cue :
" Why should I play the fool and like a Roman
Die on my sword: while there is life, there's hope,
The gashes are for them."

*Macduff.* " Turn, hell-hound, turn."

*Mr. Burbage.* I don't think Macduff ought to call Macbeth a hell-hound.

*The Producer.* What do you suggest?

*Mr. Burbage.* I should suggest : " False Monarch, turn." It's more dignified.

*Macduff.* I would rather say " hell-hound."

*The Producer.* Supposing we made it " King of Hell."

*Mr. Burbage.* I don't think that would do.

*The Producer.* Then we must leave it for the present.

*Macduff.* " Turn, hell-hound, turn."
        [*They begin to fight with wooden swords.*

*The Stage Manager.* You don't begin to fight till Macduff says " Give thee out."

*Mr. Burbage.* I think we might run those two speeches into one, and I might say :
" Of all men I would have avoided thee,
But come on now, although my soul is charged
With blood of thine, I'll have no further words.
My voice is in my sword."
Then Macduff could say :
" O bloodier villain than terms can well express."

*The Producer.* We must consult the author about that.

*Mr. Burbage.* We'll do the fencing without words first.

[*They begin to fight again.* MACDUFF *gives* MR. BURBAGE *a tremendous blow on the shoulder.*

*Mr. Burbage.* Oh ! oh ! That's my rheumatic shoulder. Please be a little more careful, Mr. Foote. You know I've got no padding. I can't go on rehearsing now. I am very seriously hurt indeed.

*Macduff.* I'm sure I'm very sorry. It was entirely an accident.

*Mr. Burbage.* I'm afraid I must go home. I don't feel up to it.

*The Stage Manager.* I'll send for some ointment. Please be more careful, Mr. Foote. Couldn't you possibly see your way to take Scene III., Mr. Burbage?

*Mr. Burbage.* I know Scene III. backwards. However, I'll just run through my speech.

*The Stage Manager.* What ? " This push will cheer me ever " ?

*Mr. Burbage* [*peevishly*]. No, not that one. You know that's all right. That tricky speech about medicine. Give me the cue.

*The Stage Manager.* " That keep her from her rest."

*Mr. Burbage.* " Cure her of that :

Canst thou not minister to a sickly mind,
Pull from the memory a booted sorrow,
Rub out the troubles of the busy brain,
And with a sweet and soothing antidote
Clean the stiff bosom of that dangerous poison
Which weighs upon the heart ? "
There, you see, word-perfect. What did I say ?

*The Stage Manager.* No, no, Mr. Burbage. It's not a booted sorrow but a *rooted* sorrow. It's not a stiff bosom but a *stuff* bosom—but here's Mr. Shakespeare.

*The Author.* I've written that speech. Shall I read it ?

*The Producer.* Please.

*Mr. Shakespeare* [*reads*]. "To-morrow, and to-morrow, and to-morrow,
Creeps in this petty pace from day to day,
To the last syllable of recorded time ;
And all our yesterdays have lighted fools
The way to dusty death. Out, out, brief candle !
Life's but a walking shadow, a poor player
That struts and frets his hour upon the stage,
And then is heard no more ; it is a tale
Told by an idiot, full of sound and fury,
Signifying nothing."

*Mr. Burbage.* Well, you don't expect me to say that, I suppose. It's a third too short. There's not a single rhyme in it. It's got nothing to do with the situation, and it's an insult to the stage. " Struts and frets " indeed ! I see there's nothing left for me but to throw up the part. You can get any one you please to play Macbeth. One thing is quite certain, I won't.

[*Exit* MR. BURBAGE *in a passion.*

*The Stage Manager* [*to the* AUTHOR]. Now you've done it.

*The Author* [*to the* PRODUCER]. You said it needn't rhyme.

*The Producer.* It's Macduff. It was all your fault, Mr. Foote.

*Lady Macbeth.* Am I to wear a fair wig or a dark wig ?

*The Producer.* Oh ! I don't know.

*The Author.* Dark, if you please. People are always saying I'm making portraits. So, if you're dark, nobody can say I meant the character for the Queen or for Mistress Mary Fytton.

*The Stage Manager.* It's no good going on now. It's all up—it's all up.

**CURTAIN**

# THE PRICE OF COAL

## By Harold Brighouse

## CHARACTERS

MARY BRADSHAW, *Jack's cousin.*
JACK TYLDESLEY, *a young miner.*
ELLEN TYLDESLEY, *his mother.*
POLLY LIVESEY, *a neighbour.*

The Scene is laid in a Lancashire colliery village.

The original Lancashire version of this play is here printed for the first time. It was freely translated into the dialect of Lanarkshire for its first performance by The Scottish Repertory Theatre, at Glasgow, on November 15, 1909, under the direction of Mr. Alfred Wareing. The cast of the first performance was as follows :

| | |
|---|---|
| MARY BROWN . . . . . | Miss Agnes Bartholomew. |
| JACK BROWN . . . . . | Mr. R. B. Drysdale. |
| ELLEN BROWN . . . . . | Miss Elspeth Dudgeon. |
| POLLY WALKER . . . . . | Miss Lola Duncan. |

# THE PRICE OF COAL

*Modern industrialism has evolved its special types, and the Lancashire collier is small and wiry. He swings a pickaxe for hours on end crouched in an impossibly small space in heated atmosphere, and physique on the grand scale is unsuited to such conditions. He takes tremendous risks as part of his daily routine. His recreations are, to a fastidious taste, coarse. He works hard under ground, and plays hard above ground. Constrained attitude is so much his second nature that he sits in perfect comfort on his haunches, in the pictured pose of the mild Hindu, his back to a wall, discussing, amongst expectoration—a long row of him—football, dogs, his last spree and his next, the police reports, women.*

*Altogether a most unpleasant person, this undersized, foul-mouthed, sporting hewer of coal—until you come to know him better, to discover his simplicity of soul, his directness, his matter-of-fact self-sacrifice, the unconscious heroism of his life : and to lose sight of his superficial frailties in your admiration for his finer qualities.*

*The womenkind of the colliers are marked by the life of the pits no less than the men. They are rough, capable housewives, dressing with more care for durability than effect, tolerant of their menfolk's weaknesses, and, above all, stamped with the pit-side stoicism apt to be mistaken for callousness. The sudden death of their breadwinner is an everyday hazard, accepted without complaint and without concealment as part of their life. Like their husbands, they exist from hand to mouth on the brink of eternity. Thrift, when any day's work may be your last, seems a misplaced virtue. Lean fare approaches as pay-day recedes, and illness, meagrely provided for by membership of a " sick " society, is tided over in the main by the unfailing generosity of neighbours whose own table suffers by the charity.*

*The Scene represents the living-room of a collier's cottage in Lancashire. The room has three doors, R., L., and C.; that at the C. leading out, the R. to the stairs, and the L. to a bedroom on the ground floor. The fireplace is R., and the window at the back with the holland blind drawn. The room contains a table (plain deal), chairs, and a comfortable rocking-chair placed by the fireplace. There is a dresser with cupboards in its lower portion and a plate-rack over it L. A bird-cage hangs in the window. Small clock, tea canister, etc., on the mantelpiece.*

[*As the curtain rises the room is in darkness, the time being 5.30 a.m. MARY BRADSHAW, a girl of about twenty, enters from the door R., goes to the gas bracket which hangs over the table, strikes a match on the box she holds in her hand and lights the gas, which has no globe. The girl is just up and not at her best. Her dark hair has been hurriedly screwed up; she has list slippers and a drab skirt. After lighting the gas she finishes fastening her print blouse, which buttons at the front. There is a small spirit-lamp on the hob, with a little tin kettle on it. She lights the lamp. Then she goes to the door L. and knocks upon it.*

*Mary.* Art oop, Jack? It's gone ha'f-past five.

*Jack* [*within*]. All reeght. A'll be there in a minute.

[MARY *takes a plain apron from a hook over the dresser and puts it on briskly, then takes a cup and saucer from the rack, putting them on the dresser, from the cupboard of which she takes a cocoa-tin and puts a spoonful of cocoa in the cup. Then she takes bread and meat from the cupboard and makes one or two huge rough sandwiches. These she puts on a plate, covers with another plate, and ties in a large red handkerchief with the ends looped for carrying. A tin can with a screw top is placed near by. Enter L. JACK TYLDESLEY, Mary's cousin, a young collier. JACK is dressed in his working or " black " clothes, which may have been coloured once but are now blackened with coal-dust. He wears no collar, but a muffler which, doffed in the pit, retains some signs of its original red shade. He is lithe and wiry but of no great stature. He carries a miner's safety-lamp in his hand, and places it on the table by the food which MARY has prepared. As he comes, MARY goes to the stove and makes his cocoa.*

*Jack.* A weren't hardly looking for to see thee this morning, Mary.

*Mary [going on with her operations at the stove].* Bless the lad, why not ? Mebbe yo'd raither A dragged thy moother out o' her bed and her wi' her rheumatics an' all.

*Jack.* A'd 'ave done for masel' for once in a way.

*Mary.* Nice mess tha'd mak' o' the job.

*Jack.* A'm not a babby.

*Mary.* A fancy A can see thee doing it an' getting to the pit behind time an' all. We've noan quarrelled, have we ?

*Jack.* Not as A knows on.

*Mary.* Then why shouldn't A get up an' do for yo', same as A have done pretty near as long as A can call to mind ?

*Jack.* A dunno.

*Mary.* No, nor any one else neither.

*Jack* [*apologetically*]. Fact is A thowt mebbe after what we was saying last neeght as yo'd noan care to see me this morning.

*Mary.* Nay, there's nowt upsettin' in that as A sees to mak' me seek owt other than what's usual.

*Jack* [*bending over her—eagerly*]. Then, wilt thou tell me——

*Mary* [*cutting him short and putting the cocoa on the table—dryly*]. There's thy cocoa. Best drink it while it's hot.

*Jack.* Aye. [*He takes a sip and puts the cup down quickly, spluttering.*] It is hot, an' all.

*Mary.* It's a cold morning to turn out into. Yo'll do wi' summat hot this weather.

*Jack.* Aye. A dessay 'tis, but weather can wait. A've summat else to talk about to thee besides weather.

*Mary.* Mebbe tha hast, my lad, an' mebbe tha'll talk about it when proper time cooms.

*Jack* [*pleadingly*]. Mary, lass, must A wait until to-neeght for an answer?

*Mary* [*drawing back*]. Play fair now, Jack. Yo' give a day from last neeght to think on it.

*Jack.* A know A did. That's reeght enough. Only waiting's not so blamed easy as A thowt when it cooms to doing it.

*Mary.* Happen it's not. But tha'll have to put up wi' it. Waiting were thy notion. A didn't ask for it.

*Jack* [*appealingly*]. Don't be hard on a chap, Mary. A want thee that bad, lass, A'm on pricks till A know which road cat's going to jump. Tha never knows what's a-going to chance down in pit. Think, lass. A might never coom up again and tha'd be sick an' sorry if A were blowed to kingdom come wi'out the consolation o' knowing tha meant to have me.

*Mary.* No, tha don't, my lad. Tha'll not frighten me that road. A'm noan pit-born like yo', but A've lived alongside pits too long for that. And tha knows very well it's noan reeght to talk about them things. A towld thee A'd give thee thy answer to-neeght an' tha'll bide till to-neeght for it. A'm noan going back on my word.

*Jack.* But if tha knows what tha's going to say why can't tha tell me now and put me out o' my misery?

*Mary.* Aye, an' have thee going round telling folks tha'd nobbut to whistle an' A rushed into thy arms. No, my lad, A'm a single woman yet an' A'm noan promised to any man. A'll tak' my own time to tell thee whether A'm game to change my name or not. [*Breaking off and looking at clock*] It's time tha was flitting. Tha'll be late if tha doan't get a move on.

*Jack* [*sullenly*]. A doan't care if A am.

*Mary.* Yes, tha dost. Tha's no need to turn stupid. Tha's noan missed being in first cage down sin' tha's bin going to pit, an' A'll noan have it said tha started missing through me. Hast finished thy cocoa?

*Jack* [*drinking it up*]. Aye. Tha's rare an' hard on a chap, Mary.

*Mary.* Get along wi' thee. If tha'd bin as hot on for weddin' me as tha reckons thasel', mebbe tha'd have upped an' asked me a bit sooner.

*Jack* [*protestingly*]. A nobbut waited while my mind were mad' oop proper. A asked thee sharp enough when it were.

*Mary.* Then tha'll wait while mine's made oop. What's sauce for th' goose is sauce for th' gander.

*Jack.* Yo' couldn't give me so much as an 'int now? Nobbut a lick an' a promise like?

*Mary.* Nay, A'm makking no promises till A'm ready. Tha's only wasting thy time and chancing being late, an' all.

*Jack* [*resignedly*]. Eh well, if A mun wait, A mun wait.

*Mary.* Evening 'ull coom before tha knows it.

*Jack* [*going to door* L. *and taking his cap from a peg in the door*]. Oh aye. Talking's easy. Yo're nobbut having me on a piece o' string all time, tha teasing wench. It's mebbe fun to thee, but it's no ways fun to me carrying on wilful like that. [*Putting his cap on.*

*Mary* [*threateningly*]. Tha'll mak' thyself late for thy work. That's what's going to be th' end of it.

*Jack.* All reeght. A'm going. Where's my baggin'?

[MARY *hands the handkerchief of food and the can,
    which he slings over his shoulder by a short strap
    attached to it.*

*Mary.* There tha art.

*Jack.* Hast wrapped 'un oop well?

*Mary.* Aye. Why?

*Jack.* Rats was busy at 'un yesterday when A coom to put my pick down an' feel for my dinner. But yo' canna help rats in a pit, an' happen they're as hungry as A am.

*Mary.* Well, it's made up as fast as A can get it. [*Looking at clock*] Now look sharp or tha'll be late.

[JACK *turns to go.*

Tha's forgetting thy lamp. Wheerever would'st be if A weren't oop to look after thee?

*Jack.* It's wi' thinking of thee, lass.

[*Taking the lamp.*

*Mary.* Time enough for that when thy shift's over.

*Jack* [*at the door* C.]. A'll be whoam pretty sharp when it is, so tha'd best be ready.

*Mary.* A'll be ready reeght enough.

*Jack.* All reeght. Then we'll leave it at that.

*Mary.* Aye.                              [*Exit* JACK.

[MARY *holds the door open and stands for a mo-
    ment watching him go. He turns in the direc-
    tion remote from the window. Morning is
    breaking, and the first grey light is visible
    through the door. She closes it and then draws
    the blind up: as she does so,* ELLEN TYLDES-
    LEY, JACK'S *mother, enters through the door* R.
    *She is an old woman, spare in figure, and bear-
    ing the signs of a hard life. She is dressed*

*plainly in black.* MARY *starts round in surprise from the blind as the door opens.*

[*Going towards her*] Why, aunt, you're up early.

*Ellen* [*standing by the door*]. Aye. Has the lad gone?

*Mary.* He's nobbut just gone out. Is anything the matter?

*Ellen.* No, lass, no. A'd a fancy to see him afore he went, that's all.

*Mary.* Shall A run after him? He's only just this minute gone.

*Ellen.* An' mak' him late? No, we munna do that. It were nobbut a fancy. A thowt as A might catch him, but A'll noan chance makking him late. He tak's a pride in being there reg'lar for first cage down, an' he'd be rare an' mad wi' me if A called 'un back for nowt.

*Mary.* Why didn't yo' shout us from your room?

*Ellen.* A didn't think to.

*Mary* [*puzzled but consoling*]. Well A'm sorry tha left thy bed for nothing, before the room's aired too.

*Ellen.* That's nowt, lass.

*Mary* [*briskly*]. Well, sit thee down while A mak' fire an' get the breakfast ready. Room 'ull soon be warm.

*Ellen* [*absently*]. Aye, lass.

[ELLEN *moves listlessly across and sits passively in the rocking-chair.* MARY *takes some sticks and paper out of the oven and kneels to make a fire.*

*Mary.* It's a bit sharp this morning, too.

[*Without turning, she goes on with her fire, lighting the sticks and putting on coal.*

[ELLEN *does not reply, but puts a handkerchief to her eyes.* MARY *gets up smartly and turns, seeing* ELLEN'S *distress.*

Aunt, what is it? Won't yo' tell me what's troubling you?

*Ellen.* Nowt, lass, nowt.

*Mary.* But there must be summat. What made yo'

get oop so early? Yo' were sleeping sound enough when A left you.

*Ellen.* Sleeping? Aye, A were sleeping reeght enough, an' would to God A weren't.

*Mary.* What dost mean?

*Ellen.* Only an owd woman's fancy, lass.

*Mary.* No. Yo' mun tell me what it is.

*Ellen.* Tha'll nobbut laugh at me.

*Mary.* No, no, A shan't. What were it?

*Ellen.* It were a dream as got me oop, lass.

*Mary.* A dream!

*Ellen.* Aye. [*Becoming increasingly terrified as she relates her dream*] A dreamed A were going in a field and the grass were green, greener than life, and theer was cows in it an' sheep—not dirty, blackened beasties same as they are wi' us, but like as yo' might fancy they'd be soomwheer where theer isn't allays smoke. And A walked in th' field, and the sun were shining, an' it come dark sudden and A couldn't see the cows no more. Theer were thunder an' it frightened me; an' when A come to look up again it were raining blood on my yead. Nowt but blood, and the field ran red wi' it. Blood everywheer. Nowt but blood.

*Mary* [*sympathetically but relieved to find it no worse*]. An' it frightened thee? Aye, th' neeghtmare's noan pleasant for anybody. Yo' did eat a bit hearty last neeght. Well, never mind, it's all ower now. Tha'll feel better after a cup of tea. A'll soon have breakfast on table now.

*Ellen* [*impressively, but as if to herself rather than addressing* MARY]. A've dreamed yon dream afore, an' the last time as A dreamed it were the neeght afore the big fire in the pit when Jack's father got 'isself killed. A've noan dreamed it sin' that neeght, and now it's coom again an' my boy's gone out to his work an' me too late to stop 'un.

*Mary* [*rushing to door* C.]. Mebbe it's not too late.

*Ellen* [*as if awakened*]. Coom back, lass. [*Looking*

*at clock*] Look at clock. First cage 'ull be going down long afore tha could get theer, and our Jack 'ull be in it. He's allays in first cage is our Jack. Best time-keeper on the pit.

*Mary* [*distractedly*]. Oh, why didn't yo' tell me at onct ? He'll be killed ; he'll be killed.

*Ellen* [*calmly*]. It's no use taking on like that. Jack's in God's keeping, lass, same as he is every day whether A dream or A don't. An' A dunno as theer's owt to trouble for. Folks do say as theer's nowt in dreams. A doubt it's going against th' Almighty to tak' notice of a dream : if He'd meant it for a warn-ing, He'd happen 'ave sent it sooner so as A could have stopped Jack going out.

*Mary* [*calmed a little*]. Aye, he's in God's keeping. We can do nowt.

*Ellen* [*briskly*]. Now. We're nowt but a pair o' silly wimmen to get skeered o' a dream. Don't thee take on about my whimsies. Coom now, bustle about. We'll never have breekfast to-day this road. Get kettle filled.

*Mary.* Yes, aunt.

*Ellen* [*rising*]. A'll see to table.

*Mary.* All reeght.

[ELLEN *takes a coarse white cloth from a drawer in the table and spreads it, putting on it two cups and saucers, plates, and a brown teapot. MARY meantime lifts the kettle from the hob and goes out R. The sound of water pouring into the kettle is heard, and MARY returns and puts the kettle on the fire.*

*Ellen.* Put gas out, lass. It's leeght enough without now. [MARY *turns gas out.* ELLEN *sits before the fire. Reminiscently*] Yo'll hardly mind an accident here, will yo', Mary ?

*Mary.* No.

*Ellen.* No. A thowt not. It's many a year sin' theer were 'un to speak of. A doan't call to mind as

A've yeard the alarm bell ring more than onct or
mebbe twict sin' your uncle were killed. [*With pride*]
That were summat like a do. Theer was about twenty
killed that time, an' a matter o' forty or more as were
hurt. Biggest accident as ever was in these parts
were that 'un. A've yeard folks say as theer 'ave bin
bigger do's in America, but A doan't tak' much notice
o' them noospaper tales masel'. Eh, it might a' bin
yesterday.

*Mary* [*sitting on the floor at* ELLEN'S *feet*]. Tell me
about it, aunt. You've never towld me how it
chanced.

*Ellen.* Eh? Bless the lass, what's good o' that?
[*With energy*] Seems to me we're both on us a bit
crocked to-day. We's got accident on the brain.

*Mary* [*trying to draw her*]. They allays ring the bell,
doan't they, aunt, when theer's owt goes wrong?

*Ellen.* Not for an odd man an' 'is butty nipped in
a roof-fall; only if it's a big thing. [*Pulling herself up*]
Sithee, lass, if tha canna talk o' nowt bar accidents,
tha'd best shut thy faice. What wi' my dream an'
thy worriting, A dunno wheer A am.

*Mary.* A were only asking. Theer's never no knowing wi' a coal-pit when it's going to turn awkward,
an' a man canna remember allays wheer he is when
he's down.

*Ellen.* They're watched sharper going down nowadays, and the fellers knows better nor to tak' risks
theirselves like they'd used to in th' ould days.

*Mary.* Aye. But a man as forgets onct 'ull forget
onct too often.

*Ellen* [*sharply*]. A've towld thee to quit moither-
ing. Folks 'ud think tha'd noan lived aside pits
beyond a week to hear thee talk silly like that.
Theer's allays danger, an' no one bar a born fool 'ud
say theer warn't, but it won't mend it to goa thinking
on't. Coal's theer and coal's got to be gotten, and
that's top and bottom of it. Hast put tea in th' pot?

*Mary.* Naw [*rising*].

*Ellen.* Tha'd best do it, then.

    [MARY *puts tea in the teapot from a canister on the mantelpiece. As she does so, a bell outside is heard ringing violently.*

*Mary* [*dropping the canister on the table*]. What's that ?

    [*The bell rings for a few moments, and ceases before* ELLEN *speaks.*

*Ellen* [*quietly and slowly, bending her head as if to a physical blow*]. God's will be done.

*Mary.* Is it——

*Ellen* [*resignedly*]. Aye. [MARY *makes for the door.*] Wheer's tha going, lass ?

*Mary* [*stopping, surprised at the question*]. A'm going to pit to see what's to do.

*Ellen.* No, thou art not. A'll want thee here.

*Mary.* Why not ?

*Ellen* [*rising*]. Theer'll be enough fools o' wimmen theer seein' what's to do and hampering the men at theer work without yo're going and helping 'un to do it.

*Mary.* But we——

*Ellen.* Sithee, lass, if our Jack's hurt, our job's to get 'un well again. Rushing off to pit-bank 'ull do 'un no good, unless mebbe tha's wanting to goa and get thy photo took an' see thy pretty face in paper same as Jack were showing us wi' yon pit as fell in soomwheer t'other day.

*Mary.* Yo' know A'm not.

*Ellen.* No. Yon's noan our way. It's only wimmen as hasn't got husbands and sons down in th' pit as goes standing round fainting and what not and making a nuisance o' themselves. T'others stays at whoam an' gets things ready.

*Mary.* We doan't know what to get ready for.

*Ellen.* We know enough.

*Mary.* Jack may not be hurt.

*Ellen* [*dryly*]. Then us'll 'ave wasted our work.

*Mary* [*dully*]. What shall A do?

*Ellen* [*looking round the room*]. A dunno as there's so much when all's done. We'll mebbe want hot water.

*Mary* [*shuddering*]. For——

*Ellen* [*roughly*]. How do A know what for? [*Quietly looking round*] Yon kettleful 'ull do, and our tea mun bide.

*Mary* [*distractedly*]. But what can we do? Give me summat to do, for mercy's sake. A'll goa mad if A doan't stir about. A can't sit still and wait, and wait, and wait.    [*Her voice rises almost to a scream.*

*Ellen*. Tha'd best be makking his bed.

*Mary* [*breaking down, tearfully*]. Yes, aunt.

*Ellen*. What's tha crying for, lass? We doan't know nowt yet, and if we did, crying won't mend it. It 'ull do Jack no good, so how he is, to see thee slobbering when he cooms in.

[MARY *dries her eyes, sniffling, and begins to clear the table.*

What's tha doing that for?

*Mary*. A dunno. A thowt——

*Ellen*. Folks must eat. Leave things be. A towld thee to goa into his room and mak' his bed.

*Mary* [*going*]. All reeght, aunt.

[*Exit* MARY, L., *closing the door behind her.*
[ELLEN *looks to see that it is shut and then moves rapidly and purposefully to the door* C. *She throws it open. It is now daylight. The confused murmur of a distant crowd is heard. She stands on the threshold and looks out. Presently she speaks to some one approaching, but not yet visible.*

*Ellen*. What is it, Polly?

[POLLY LIVESEY, *a middle-aged woman, in clogs, drab skirt and blouse, and with a shawl over her head and shoulders, appears breathless in the doorway.*

*Polly.* Ropes slipped and cage fell down shaft. Is yours gone out to his work ?

*Ellen.* First cage down ?

*Polly.* Aye.

*Ellen.* Mine's in it.

*Polly.* We'll know worst soon. They was rigging tackle when A coom away. They'll have 'em up in no time.

*Ellen.* A'll be ready. Wheer's yours ?

*Polly.* Mine's all reeght safe in theer beds, sleeping off last neeght's fuddle, thank the Lord.

*Ellen.* They mun bring 'un here, Polly, so how he is.

*Polly.* Aye. We all like to do for our own. Wheer's the lass ? Gone to pit ?

*Ellen.* Makkin' 'is bed against he cooms.

*Polly [approvingly].* That's reeght. Doan't let her out.

*Ellen.* Not if A can help it. She wanted to goa, but A wouldna have it. Theer's sights seen at pit-mouth arter an accident as isn't fit for a young 'un. Spoil her life for her to be theer when they're browt up.

*Polly.* Aye. Am noan going back. A've had soom. Never no more if I can help it.

*Ellen.* Coom in, wilta ?

*Polly.* Aye. A'd best close door, too, and keep noise out or she'll be wanting to go.    *[Closes door.*

                                   *[The murmur ceases.*

*Ellen.* Aye. They can't sit still when they're young.

*Polly.* That's a fact. A recollect the day when the pit were afire. A were nobbut a young woman then, but my moother had no better sense nor to let me out to pit-mouth to see the bodies browt up. A'll never forget that sight. A dream of it to this day.

                   *[ELLEN *sits on the rocking-chair.*

*Ellen.* Sit thee down, Polly. A bit o' coompany cooms nicely at a time like this.

*Polly [sitting].* Thankee.

*Ellen.* Aye, it's a thing yo' canna forget. Seems as it might be only t'other day as A yeard th' ould bell clang and saw my man browt oop. He were that charred A only knowed him by the earrings as he woore because his eyes was weak. They towld me arterwards as a hare had crossed his path on his road to the pit, but he were allays obstinate, were my Joe, and he wouldna tak' warning. And now the cage has slippit wi' my son in her and A'll have no manfolk now.

[*The door* L. *opens and* MARY *stands in the doorway. The others do not see her.*

*Polly.* Tha never knows. Mebbe he'll not be killed.

*Ellen* [*hopelessly*]. A dreamt same dream last neeght as when his faither went.

*Polly* [*quite convinced that hope is futile*]. In the midst o' life we are in death. Theer's no truer word nor that.

*Ellen.* Not when yo' live by coal. Theer's wimmin as keeps house in the places th' coal goas to as pays for their coal wi' brass. We pay for it a sight heavier here. We pays wi' the lives o' men.

*Polly* [*consoling her*]. But it's a comfort to think he'll noan be burned. A can't abide a corse that's burnt.

*Ellen* [*agreeing*]. Aye, better broke than burnt.

*Polly.* And tha'll have money in the burial club.

*Ellen.* Oh aye. A can bury 'un proper.

*Polly.* That's allays a comfort. Yo' doan't somehow seem to care so much when yo' know 'un's had a proper funeral. He's bin a good son to yo', an' all.

*Ellen.* Oh aye, he's a good lad. He's mebbe had his shilling on a horse now and again and gone rattin' of a Sunday morning, but that's nobbut to say he's a man and not an angel in breeches.

*Polly.* It's more than A can say wi' my lot. Lazy, drunken good-for-nowts they are, faither and sons alike. Coom to mention it, it's a rum thing. Providence goes to work its own way. If mine hadna bin on spree last neeght they'd as like as not have bin in cage along o' your Jack.

*Mary* [*quietly*]. A'll go to pit now, aunt.

[*She moves towards door* C.

*Ellen.* Wait your hurry, lass.

*Mary.* A can't wait. A mun know.

*Ellen.* Sit thee down.

*Mary* [*feverishly*]. A can't sit down and hearken to yo' pair talking that road. First yo' get 'un killed and then yo' bury 'un, and next thing yo'll be debating what's to goa on's gravestone, and all the time yo' doan't so much as know if he's hurt.

*Polly.* Sit thee still, lass. Tha'd best wait.

*Mary.* Oh, A dunno what yo're made of, yo' two. Yo' sit theer quiet and calm as if theer weren't nowt the matter.

*Ellen.* We're owd enough to know we canna do no good. Hast made bed oop?

*Mary.* Aye.

*Ellen.* Well, theer's a bottle o' brandy in th' cupboard in my room. We might need 'un.

*Mary.* A'll get it. [*Goes off briskly* R.

*Polly.* She's getting restless.

*Ellen.* Aye. It cooms harder when yo're young to keep thasel' to thasel'. It doan't coom natural to her, not being born to pits, same as we was. Her moother was wed to a weaver chap in Blackburn and browt her oop to factories. It taks above a year or two to get into th' way o' the pits when yo're born foreign.

*Polly.* Aye. We're used to thowt o' losing our men sudden.

*Ellen.* But she's noan going to pit-mouth if A can stop her. We mun keep her a-gait. Is theer owt else we might want as yo' can think on?

*Polly.* A dunno as theer is.

*Ellen.* We might want linen fur tying up.

*Polly.* No, yo' winna. Doctors was theer afore A coom away, and ambulance chaps, too, wi' all as they'll want. But we mun keep her here so how she likes it.

*Ellen.* Aye [*looking at door* c.].

[POLLY *follows her example and then looks at* ELLEN.

Dost mind ? A doan't move so easy as A used.

*Polly.* The door ?

*Ellen.* Aye.

*Polly.* Aye. That's reeght [*getting up and going to door*]. Better let her think tha's treating her bad than let her out to see them sights.

[*She locks the door and gives* ELLEN *the key, then resumes her seat.*

*Ellen.* Thankee, Polly. [*She pockets the key.*] Help me to mak' talk now and keep her mind off it.

[*Enter* MARY, R., *with the brandy.*]

*Mary.* Here's brandy.           [*Puts it on the table.*

*Ellen.* That's reeght.

[*A slight pause. The old women try to make conversation. First* POLLY *bobs forward in her seat as if about to speak, but leans back without saying anything.* ELLEN *repeats Polly's performance.* MARY *moves towards the door.* ELLEN *glances round desperately for a subject and hits on the brandy bottle, bringing out her remark in time to arrest* MARY'S *progress before she reaches the door.*

A thowt theer were more in th' bottle than that, too.

*Polly* [*grateful for the opening*]. It's a handy thing to have about the house.

*Ellen.* Aye. Rare stuff for th' jaw-ache.

*Polly.* It is that. Goes well wi' a cup of tea on a cowld morning, an all.

*Mary.* Is there owt else ?

*Ellen.* Eh ? No, A dunno as theer is, Mary.

[MARY *moves towards the door.*

Let me think, now.           MARY *stops again.*

Naw, that's all as A can think on.

*Mary* [*quietly*]. A'll goa now, then.

*Ellen.* Naw, tha'll not.

*Mary.* Why not, aunt ?

*Ellen.* Because tha'll not. Tha'll stay wheer tha art.

*Mary.* Let me go. A must go. A can't stay here.

*Polly.* Do what thy aunt tells thee, lass. Young folks grows that bold nowadays, theer's no telling them out.

*Mary.* Oh, yo' dunno understand. A must go. A must. [*Goes to door and tries it ; looking round surprised.*] Door's locked. [*Tries it again.*] This door's locked. [*Looks up.*] Wheer's the key ? What have yo' done with the key ?

*Ellen.* Sithee, lass, A towld thee tha'd not goa and A've made sur on't. Coom now. Coom and sit quiet and quit raving about like a mad thing. Tha'll have handle off door.

*Mary* [*still pulling at the handle*]. Let me go to him.

*Ellen.* Naw.

*Mary* [*wildly—still at the door*]. A must goa. A must. A love him. A love him.

*Ellen* [*rising*]. Dost think A doan't love him, lass ? Aye, and a sight better than a bit o' a lass like yo' could love 'un. [*Proudly*] A'm his moother.

*Mary* [*going towards her*]. Oh, have mercy. Yo' don't know. A sent him out. He weren't for going till A'd spoke th' word. A wouldna tell him ; A made him wait for evening. A sent him to his death.

*Ellen.* The girl's raving.

*Mary.* Let me go.

*Ellen.* Naw.

*Mary.* Yo' won't ?

*Polly.* Hold thy hush, lass. It's for thy own good.

*Mary.* Why have yo' locked yon door ? Yo're cheating me. Yo're cruel. A can't do no good here. Let me go to him. A must go. A will.

[*Approaching* ELLEN : *the two women face each other for a moment. Suddenly there is a loud kicking at the door.*

[*Whispering hoarsely*] What's that ? Oh, my God, what's that ?

[ELLEN *takes the key from her pocket and slowly moves to the door. She inserts the key and throws door open.* JACK *stands on the door-step, his coat buttoned at the bottom and with his right arm thrust into it.*

*Ellen.* My lad.        [*She tries to embrace him.*

*Jack* [*holding her off with his left arm*]. Steady on, moother. Mind my arm.

*Ellen.* Is't broke ?

*Jack.* Aye. Doctor'll be round to set 'un soon. They've gotten enough to do first, though. Theer's plenty worse than me.

[*He comes in and sits in the rocking-chair.*

*Ellen.* Thank God !

[*She covers her face with her hands.*

*Jack.* Nay, moother. It's all ower. Theer's nowt to cry for, and not so much in a brokken arm to thank God for, neither. [*He puts his uninjured hand upon her shoulder.*] Well, lass [*looking at* MARY].

*Mary.* Oh, Jack !

*Jack.* Is that all as tha's got to say to me ? Shift's ower, lass. Mebbe it's ower afore it's begun, but that'll noan matter. A've coom fur my answer, lass.

*Mary.* Tha owld soft. Tha knew all time. Oh, Jack, Jack, A thowt tha was killed.

*Jack.* Tha thowt wrong. A'm noan th' dying sort. So tha'll have me.

*Mary.* Aye.

*Jack.* A'll goa round an' see parson about putting up th' banns when my arm's set. A'll be having soom time on my hands. A reckon getting wed 'ull fill 'un in nicely.

**CURTAIN**

# ALLISON'S LAD

## By Beulah Marie Dix

*Allison's Lad* was originally produced by the American Academy of Dramatic Arts at the Carnegie Lyceum, New York, on December 23, 1910.

## ORIGINAL CAST

| | |
|---|---|
| COLONEL SIR WILLIAM STRICKLAND | Abner W. Cassidy. |
| CAPTAIN GEORGE BOWYER . . . | James W. Mott. |
| LIEUT. ROBERT GORING . . . . | Gerald Quina. |
| *(of the Cavalier Party)* | |

| | |
|---|---|
| FRANCIS HOPTON . . . . . | Sidney K. Powell. |
| TOM WINWOOD . . . . . | Donald Macdonald. |
| *(Gentlemen Volunteers)* | |

| | |
|---|---|
| COLONEL JOHN DRUMMOND . . . | Le Roy Clemens. |
| *(of the Roundhead Party)* | |

This play has not previously been published in England.

# ALLISON'S LAD

SCENE.—*The village of Faringford, in the western midlands of England.*

PERIOD.—*The close of the Second Civil War, autumn 1648.*

*It is midnight of a cheerless autumn day, with a drizzle of slow rain. In an upper chamber of the village inn of Faringford, lit by guttering candles and a low fire that smoulders on the hearth, are gathered five gentlemen of the Cavalier party, made prisoners that morning in a disastrous skirmish.*

*In a great arm-chair by the hearth, at stage left, sits their leader,* SIR WILLIAM STRICKLAND. *He is a tall, keen man of middle age, of the finest type of his party, a gallant officer and a high-souled gentleman. He has received a dangerous wound in the side, which has been but hastily dressed, and he now leans heavily in his chair, with eyes closed, almost oblivious of what goes on about him.*

*His captain, and friend of long standing,* GEORGE BOWYER, *a sanguine, stalwart gentleman of* STRICKLAND'S *own years, has planted himself in the centre of the room, where he is philosophically smoking at a long pipe, while he watches the play at the rude table, which stands at the stage right.*

*Round the table, on rough stools,* GORING, HOPTON, *and* WINWOOD *sit dicing and smoking, with a jug of ale between them for the cheering of their captivity.* GORING *is a swaggering young soldier of fortune;* HOPTON, *a gentleman of the Temple, turned soldier, with something of*

*the city fop still to be traced in his bearing.    He has been
wounded, and bears about his forehead a blood-flecked
bandage.   WINWOOD, the third gamester, is a mere lad of
seventeen, smooth-faced, comely, with a gallant carriage.*

*It is to be noted that the men play but half-heartedly.
Indeed, the cheerlessness of the midnight hour, in the dim
chamber, with the rain tapping on the mullioned windows, may well bring home to them the dubiousness of
their captive state and set them to anxious question of
what the dawn may have in store.   GORING, of the three
the most hardened and professionally a soldier, is the
first to speak, as he throws the dice.*

*Goring.* Cinq and tray!

*Winwood.* The main is yours, Rob Goring.

*Goring.* That's a brace of angels you owe me, Frank
Hopton.

*Hopton.* Go ask them of the scurvy Roundhead had
the stripping of my pockets.

*Bowyer [with the good-humoured contempt of the pro-
fessional for the amateur].* The more fool you to bear
gold about you when you ride into a fight!

*Winwood.* The devil fly off with the money!   The
rebels have taken my horse—a plague rot them!

*Goring.* Faith, I'd care not, if the prick-eared
brethren had not got me, and got me fast.   'Tis your
throw, Tom Winwood.

[WINWOOD *takes the dice-box, but pauses, anxiously
            awaiting an answer to* HOPTON'S *next question.*

*Hopton.* What think you, Captain Bowyer?   Are
they likely to admit us speedily to ransom?

[BOWER *shakes his head, smiling, half indifferent.*

*Goring.* You're swift to grumble, Frank.   You've
not been yet ten hours a prisoner.   Throw, Tom, a
wildfire burn you!

*Winwood [casting the dice].* There, then!   And ven-
geance profitable gaming!   We can't muster four
farthings amongst us.

*Goring.* Curse it, man, we play for love and sport.
I've never yet had enough of casting the dice. Look
you [*casts the dice*], I better you by three.

*Winwood.* On my life, no ! I threw a tray and a
quatre.

*Goring.* Go to with your jesting ! You mean a tray
and deuce !

*Winwood.* Tray and quatre I threw.

*Goring* [*starts to his feet, with his hands leaping to
draw the sword which, as a prisoner, he no longer wears*].
Will you give me the lie in my teeth ?

*Winwood* [*pluckily springs to his feet, with the same
impulse*]. Ay, if you say I threw——

> [*At the sound of the angry voices and of the stools
> thrust back,* STRICKLAND *opens his eyes and
> glances towards the brawlers.*

*Bowyer* [*laying a heavy hand upon a shoulder of each*].
Hold your tongues, you shuttle-headed fools !

> [*Thrusts* GORING *down into his seat.*

*Hopton.* You'll rouse the Colonel, and he ill and
wounded. Sit you down again !

*Winwood* [*dropping sullenly into his place*]. Yet
'twas a tray and quatre.

*Goring.* Frank, you saw the cast. A tray and
deuce, and I will so maintain it.

> [*The three at table talk heatedly in dumb show,*
> HOPTON *playing the peacemaker, until at last he
> wins the disputants to shake hands. Meantime*
> BOWYER *has gone anxiously to* STRICKLAND'S
> *side.*

*Bowyer.* How is it with you, Will, old lad ? Your
wound is easier ?

*Strickland.* My wound ? 'Tis nothing, I tell you.

*Bowyer.* Why, then, take heart ! Matters might
well be worse.

> [*He takes a candle from the chimneypiece, and re-
> lights his pipe.*

*Strickland.* Cold comfort, George !

*Bowyer.* We are defeated—prisoners—yes, I grant you. Yet we have fought our best. And for the future—by this light, our enemies have used us handsomely so far ! No doubt they'll speedily accept of ransom.

*Strickland* [*with eyes fixed on* WINWOOD]. From my heart I hope so !

*Bowyer.* Aye, to be taken thus in his first fight 'tis pity for little Tom Winwood.

*Strickland.* You say——

*Bowyer.* 'Tis of the lad yonder you are thinking.

*Strickland.* Yes, I was thinking of Allison's lad.

[*As the result of* HOPTON'S *persuasion,* WINWOOD *at that moment is most heartily drinking a health to* GORING.

*Bowyer.* My cousin Allison's boy. Look but upon him now ! A half-minute agone he and Rob Goring were ready to fly at each other's throats, and now they drink good fellowship together. Faith, by times young Tom is monstrous like unto his father.

*Strickland.* Your pardon ! Tom is his mother's son, Allison's lad every inch of him—every thought of him. There's no taint of the father in the boy.

*Bowyer.* Yes, I wonder not that you speak thus of Jack Winwood. 'Twas a damnable trick he served you when he won Allison from you with his false tales.

*Strickland.* Ay, and well-nigh broke her heart thereafter with his baseness. You stood beside me, George, there at Edgehill, when we looked upon the death-wound—in his back !

*Bowyer.* Poor wretch ! Gallant enough at the charge, but at two o'clock in the morning he'd no more courage than——

*Strickland.* He was a coward, and false from first to last. For God's sake, George, never say that boy is like his father ! For his mother's sake——

*Bowyer.* Ay, 'twould go near to killing Allison, should Tom prove craven.

*Strickland.* He'll never prove craven. He's his mother's son. Let be, George! I'm in no mood for speech.

[BOWYER *goes back to the table, where* WINWOOD, *in the last minutes, has played with notable listlessness and indifference.*

*Hopton.* 'Tis your cast, Tom.

*Winwood.* Nay, but I'm done.

*Goring.* Will you give over?

*Winwood.* But for a moment. My pipe is out.

[*Rises and goes to* STRICKLAND.

*Hopton.* Come, Captain! In good time! Bear a hand with us.

[BOWYER *sits in* WINWOOD'S *place at table, and dices.*

*Winwood.* You called me, sir?

*Strickland.* I did not call, but I was thinking of you. Sit you down.

[WINWOOD *sits on a stool at the opposite side of the hearth, and cleans and fills his pipe.*

*Strickland.* I watched you to-day, Tom. You bore yourself fairly in the fight. I was blithe to see it.

*Winwood.* God willing, you'll see better in the next fight, sir.

*Strickland.* Go to! You did all that might be asked of a youth for the first time under fire.

*Winwood.* Ah, but 'twas my second time under fire, sir.

*Strickland.* Second time? How's that, my boy?

*Winwood.* Last June, faith, I was at Bletchingley when we held the house four hours against the rebels, my schoolfellow Lord Bletchingley, and I, and the servants. I came by a nick in the arm there. I still have the scar to show.

[*Rises eagerly and puts back his sleeve to show the scar.*

*Strickland* [*lightly*]. 'Twas right unfriendly of you,

(2,797)                                                          6

Tom, to keep me so in the dark touching your exploits.

*Winwood* [*half embarrassed with the sense of having said too much, turns from* STRICKLAND *and lights his pipe with the candle that he takes from the chimney-piece*]. Truth, sir, I was shamed to speak to you of Bletchingley.

*Strickland.* Shamed ?   What do you talk of ?

*Winwood.* Why, our fight at Bletchingley; it must seem mere child's play unto you, a tried soldier, my father's old comrade. [*He speaks the word "father" with all the proper pride that a son should show.*]

*Strickland.* But your mother. She would have been proud to know that you had borne you well in the fight. You should have told her, Tom.

*Winwood* [*in swift alarm*]. Told my mother ?   Why sir, she—would have been troubled.   Perchance she would not have heard of my going out for the King with you, because of Bletchingley.

*Strickland.* Why because of Bletchingley ?

*Winwood.* Why ?   Well, you see, sir—sure, 'twas there I had this wound.

[*Re-seats himself on the stool opposite* STRICKLAND.

*Strickland.* And for that you think she would have kept you from the field ?   Lad, you do not altogether know your mother.

[BOWYER, *at the end of a talk in dumb show with* GORING *and* HOPTON, *has risen, and now goes out at the single door, wide and heavy, that leads from the chamber centre back to the outer corridor.   At the sound of the closing of the door* STRICKLAND *starts.*

*Strickland.* What was that ?

*Goring* [*rises and salutes*]. 'Twas Captain Bowyer, sir, went into the outer room to speak with the sentries. [*Re-seats himself.*

*Hopton.* Heaven send he get them to talk !   I'd fain know what's to become of us.

*Goring* [*stretching himself*]. Go sleep, like a wise man, and cease your fretting.

[*He presently rests his head on his folded arms, which he places on the table, and goes to sleep.*

*Strickland*. Sound advice, Tom ! You were best take it.

*Winwood* [*smoking throughout*]. Sleep ? How can I, sir ? I would it were day. I hate this odd and even time o' night. What think you will come of us ?

*Strickland*. What matters it, boy ? We have fought our fight, and you bore yourself gallantly, Tom.

*Winwood*. Easy to do, sir, in the daylight, with your comrades about you, but this—this waiting in the dark ! God ! I would it were day. At two in the morning I've no more courage than——

*Strickland* [*in sharp terror*]. Tom ! Hold your peace !

[BOWYER *comes again into the room.* HOPTON *springs eagerly to his fret.*

*Hopton*. What news, Captain ?

*Bowyer*. Bad. They're quitting the village this same hour.

*Goring*. A retreat by night ?

[*Rises and confers in dumb show with* HOPTON.

*Bowyer*. Your wound cannot endure this hasty moving, Will. In mere humanity they must let you rest here at the inn. You'll give them your parole.

*Strickland*. You'll talk to your captors of paroles, after so many paroles have been broken by men that are a shame unto our party ?

*Bowyer*. But you are known for a man of honour. And by happy chance the colonel in command of these rebels has come hither within the hour. He will listen to me. I knew him of old—one John Drummond.

*Winwood*. Drummond !

[*His hand clenches convulsively upon his pipe, which snaps sharply under the pressure.*

[COLONEL DRUMMOND *enters the room. He is a*

*grave, stern gentleman of middle age, in military
dress, with cuirass, and sword at side.* WIN-
WOOD, *at his entrance, shifts his position so that
his back is towards him, and sits thus, with head
bent and hands tight clenched.*

*Bowyer.* In good time, Colonel Drummond !

*Drummond [throughout with the fine dignity of a
soldier and a gentleman].* I fear not, Captain. There
are three of you here in presence with whom I must
have a word. [*Seats himself at table.*] Lieutenant
Goring !

*Goring [with some swagger].* Well, sir ?

*Drummond.* At Raglan Castle you gave your promise never again to bear arms against the Parliament.
Now that you are taken with arms in your hands, have
you aught to say in your defence ?

*Goring.* Before I gave that promise to your damned
usurping Parliament, I swore to serve the King. I
keep the earlier oath.

*Drummond.* And for that you will answer in this
hour. Now you, Mr. Hopton ?

*Bowyer.* Frank Hopton, too ?

*Drummond.* What defence is yours for your breach
of parole ?

*Hopton.* It was forced from me. A forced promise,
faith, 'tis void in the courts of law.

*Drummond.* It may well be, but not in a court
of war.

*Strickland.* George ! Did he say there were—three
had broken faith ?

*Drummond.* And now for you, Thomas Winwood !

[WINWOOD *starts to his feet but does not face*
DRUMMOND.

*Bowyer.* Tom, not you !

*Drummond.* Last June, at Bletchingley, you, sir,
gave to me personally your word of honour never
again to take up arms——

*Strickland [rising for the moment as if unwounded,*

*with all his strength*]. Face that scoundrel! Face him and tell him that he lies!

*Winwood* [*unwillingly turns and faces* DRUMMOND, *but tammers when he tries to speak*]. I—I——

*Strickland.* Speak out!

*Drummond.* Well, Mr. Winwood?

*Strickland.* Answer! The truth! The truth! Have you broken your parole?

*Winwood* [*desperately at bay, with his back to the wall, his comely young face for the moment the face of his coward and trickster father*]. God's death! I've done no more than a hundred others have done. They've not kept faith with us, the cursed rebels. Why the fiend's name should we keep faith with them? It was a forced promise. And the King—I was fain to serve him, as my father served him, like my father——

*Strickland.* Like your father! [*He staggers where he stands, a wounded man, a sick man—mortally sick at heart.*] Allison's lad!

*Bowyer* [*catching* STRICKLAND *as he staggers*]. Will!

*Strickland* [*masters himself and stands erect*]. Let be! Colonel Drummond, I ask your pardon for my words a moment since. I could not believe—I could not believe—— [*He sinks upon his chair.*] He is his father's son, George! His father's son.

*Drummond.* Come here, Winwood!

[*Heavily* WINWOOD *goes across the room and halts by the table, but throughout he keeps his dazed and miserable eyes on* STRICKLAND.

*Drummond.* You realize well, the three of you, that by the breaking of your paroles you have forfeited your lives unto the Parliament.

*Hopton.* Our lives? You've no warrant——

*Drummond* [*laying his hand upon the hilt of his sword*]. I have good warrant—here. I was minded first to stand the three of you against the wall in the court below and have you shot in the presence of your misguided followers.

*Bowyer.* Colonel Drummond, I do protest !

*Drummond.* You waste your words, sir.   This hour I purpose to give a lesson to all the promise-breakers of your party.

*Goring.* You purpose, then, to butcher us, all three ?

*Drummond.* Your pardon !   Two of you I shall admit to mercy.   The third——

*Hopton.* Well !   Which of us is to be the third ?

*Drummond.* You may choose by lot which one of you shall suffer.   You have dice here.   Throw, and he who throws the lowest——

*Hopton* [*with a burst of half hysterical laughter*]. Heaven's light, Rob, for once ye'll have enough of casting the dice !

*Drummond.* Winwood, you are the youngest.   You shall throw first.   Winwood !

[WINWOOD *stands as if dazed, his eyes still on* STRICKLAND.

*Goring.* Are you gone deaf, Tom Winwood ?

*Winwood* [*thrusts out a groping hand*]. I—I—— Give me the dice !

*Hopton* [*putting the dice-box into* WINWOOD'S *hand*]. Here !   Be quick !

[*A moment's pause, while* WINWOOD, *with twitching face, shakes the box and shakes again.*

*Goring.* For God's love, throw !

*Winwood* [*throws, uncovers dice, and averts his eyes*]. What is it ?

*Drummond.* Seven is your cast.   You, Hopton !

[*Feverishly* HOPTON *snatches the box, shakes, and casts quickly.*

*Drummond.* Eleven !

*Hopton* [*almost hysterically*].   God be thanked for good luck !   God be thanked !

*Goring.* Damn you !   Hold your tongue !

[HOPTON *snatches a cup from the table and drinks thirstily.*   GORING *throws, and holds dice for a moment covered.*

*Goring.* It's between us now, Tom!

*Winwood* [*wiping his forehead with his sleeve*]. Yes.
[GORING *uncovers the dice.*

*Drummond.* Eight!

*Goring* [*with a long breath of relief*]. Ah!

*Drummond* [*rising*]. The lot has fallen upon you,
Mr. Winwood.

*Winwood.* I am—at your disposal, sir.

*Drummond.* You have ten minutes in which to
make you ready.

*Goring.* Ten minutes!

[WINWOOD *sinks heavily into his old seat at table.*
*Presently he draws to him the dice and box, and*
*mechanically throws again and again.*

*Bowyer* [*intercepting* DRUMMOND *as he turns to*
*leave the room*]. You shall listen to me, Drummond.
The boy's my kinsman. He——

*Drummond.* Stand aside, George Bowyer!
[*He goes out of the room.*

*Bowyer* [*following* DRUMMOND *out*]. Yet you shall
listen! Drummond! Listen to me!

*Hopton.* But 'tis mere murder. 'Tis against all
law.

*Goring.* Will you prattle of law to Cromwell's men?
[*Comes to table and lays a hand on* WINWOOD'S
*shoulder.*] Tom, lad, I would we could help you.

*Winwood.* I've thrown the double six—twice. 'Tis
monstrous droll, eh, Rob? Before—I could throw
no higher than seven—no higher than seven!

[*His voice rises higher and higher, and breaks into*
*a shrill laughter.*

*Goring.* Steady! Steady, lad!

[STRICKLAND *looks up, as if rousing from a trance.*

*Hopton* [*hastily fills a cup and offers it to* WINWOOD].
Here, Tom, drink this down.

*Winwood* [*snatches the cup and starts to drink, but*
*in the act looks up and reads in his comrades' faces the*
*fear that is on them, that he is about to disgrace the colours*

*that he wears.   He sets down the cup*]. You—you
think—— Will you leave me—for these minutes?
A' God's name, let me be!

> [HOPTON *and* GORING *draw away to the window
> and stand watching* WINWOOD *anxiously.   He
> has taken up the dice-box, and again is mechani-
> cally casting the dice.*

*Hopton.*  How will he bear himself yonder?

*Goring.*  You mean——

*Hopton.*  There in the courtyard when they——

*Goring.*  Speak lower!

*Strickland* [*rises with effort, crosses, and lays his
hand on* WINWOOD'S *shoulder*].  Tom!

*Winwood* [*starting up, furiously*].  You're ashamed
of me!  You're ashamed!  Don't pity me!  Let me
be, curse you, let me be!

*Strickland* [*sternly*].  Tom!  Look at me!

*Winwood* [*turns defiantly, meets* STRICKLAND'S
*eyes, and desperately clings to them*].  I can't!  I can't!
If they'll wait till it's light—but now—in the dark—
Make them wait till morning!  I can't bear it!  I
can't bear it!

*Strickland.*  Be still!  You must face it, and face it
gallantly.

*Winwood* [*stands erect, fighting hard for self-control*].
Gallantly.  Yes.  My father—he died for the King.
I mustn't disgrace him.  I must bear myself as he
would have done.  I——

*Strickland.*  Don't speak of him!  Think on your
mother.

*Winwood.*  Must you tell her—why they shot me?
She would think of it—of that broken promise—as a
woman might.  God's life!  Why will you judge me
so?  My father would have understood.

*Strickland.*  Yes.  He would have understood you
well.

*Winwood.*  What do you mean?  I'm a coward—a
promise-breaker.  You think that.  But my father

—he died for the King. He—— [*In* STRICKLAND'S *face he reads that of which in all these years he has been kept in ignorance.*] How did my father die?

*Strickland.* Not now, Tom!

[BOWYER *comes again into the room.*

*Winwood* [*almost beside himself*]. Answer me! Answer me! Bowyer! You're my cousin. Tell me the truth! As God sees us! How did my father die? How did my father live? You won't answer? You've lied! You've lied! All of you—all these years! He was a coward. You don't deny it! A coward—a false coward—and I'm his son! I'm his son.

[*Sinks upon a stool by the table, with face hidden, and breaks into rending sobs.*

*Bowyer.* Will! Will! You can bear no more.

*Strickland* [*shakes off* BOWYER'S *arm and goes to* WINWOOD]. Stand up! Stand up! You are your mother's son as well as his!

*Winwood* [*rising blindly, as if* STRICKLAND'S *voice alone had power to lift him*]. A coward! You see. Like him. And there in the courtyard—— Ah, God! I'll break! I'll break.

*Strickland.* You will not. For her sake—for her blood that is in you—Allison's lad!

*Winwood* [*with slow comprehension*]. You—loved her!

*Strickland.* Yes. And love that part of her which is in you. And know you will bear you well unto the end.

*Winwood.* I'll—I'll—— It's not the death. It's not that. It's the moment—before the bullet—— God! If I fail—if I fail——

*Strickland.* You will not fail.

*Winwood.* You believe that? You can believe that of me?

*Strickland.* I believe that, Tom.

*Bowyer.* Will! The ten minutes are ended.

*Strickland.* So soon ! So soon !

*Bowyer.* Drummond will suffer me be with him to the last. Come, Tom, my lad !

[*Goes up, and from a chair beside the door takes a heavy military cloak—which shall thereafter serve as* WINWOOD'S *shroud. He holds it throughout so that* WINWOOD *may not mark it.*

*Winwood* [*takes his hat, and turns to* GORING *and* HOPTON, *with a pitiful effort at jauntiness*]. God be wi' you, boys ! [*Crosses, and holds out his hand to* STRICKLAND.] Sir William ! I'll—try. But—can't you help me ? Can't you help me when——

[*Clings to* STRICKLAND'S *hand.*

*Strickland.* I can help you. You shall bear you as becomes her son.

*Winwood.* Ay, sir.

*Strickland.* And I shall know it. God keep you !

*Winwood* [*faces about*]. I am ready, sir. [*Goes to door, and on the threshold wheels and stands at salute.*] You shall have news of me, Sir William !

[WINWOOD *goes out, and* BOWYER, *with the cloak, follows after him.*

*Hopton.* What did he mean ?

*Goring.* He'll die bravely, poor lad, I'll swear to that ! [STRICKLAND *sways slightly where he stands.*

*Goring.* Sir William ! You're near to swooning. Sit you down, sir.

*Strickland.* I pray you, gentlemen, for these moments do not disturb me.

[*He stands upon the hearth, erect, steady, and very still.*

*Hopton.* Truth, the man's made of stone. I thought he had loved poor Winwood as his own son.

*Goring.* Quiet, will you ? [*He removes his hat.*

*Hopton.* What——

*Goring.* Think on what's happening in the courtyard, man !

[*A moment's pause, and then from below, in the*

*rainy courtyard, is heard the report of a muffled volley.*

*Hopton.* Hark!

*Strickland* [*in an altered, remote voice*]. Well done!

*Goring.* Grant that he made a clean ending!

*Strickland* [*turns slowly, with eyes fixed before him, and the sudden smile of one who greets a friend*]. Tom! Well done, Allison's lad! [*He pitches forward.*

*Goring* [*catching* STRICKLAND *in his arms*]. Sir William! Help here, Frank!

> [*They place* STRICKLAND *in his chair.* GORING *starts to loosen his neck gear.* HOPTON *kneels and lays his hand on* STRICKLAND'S *heart. On the moment* BOWYER *comes swiftly into the room.*

*Bowyer.* Will! Will! The lad died gallantly. He went as if a strong arm were round him.

*Hopton* [*lets fall the hand that he had laid on* STRICKLAND'S *heart. Speaks in an awe-struck voice*]. Perhaps there was!

*Goring* [*rises erect from bending over* STRICKLAND]. Captain! Sir William——

> [BOWYER *catches the note in* GORING'S *voice, and removes his hat, as he stands looking upon what he now knows to be the dead body of his friend and leader.*

CURTAIN

# THE OLD BULL

## By Bernard Gilbert

# CHARACTERS

CHARLES ELMITT, *son of the lately dead farmer, Ernest Elmitt ; age* 26.

JAMES ELMITT, *brother to Charles ; age* 24.

WILLIAM SMITHSON, *their uncle, an auctioneer and publican ; age* 56.

TOM BONES, *farm foreman at the Elmitts' ; age* 64.

SARAH TINSLEY, *housekeeper at the Elmitts' ; age* 61.

The play takes place in the Elmitts' kitchen, in the village of Pantacks.

# THE OLD BULL

*Extract from County Directory*

PANTACKS, a village of 412 inhabitants, on the main
road from Bly to Barkston. Christopher Harbord,
Esquire (Pantacks Manor), is sole landowner. The
parish is drained by Pantacks Delph, which runs into the
Old Cut. Church—St. Giles. Vicar—Rev. K. Treffry.
Wesleyan Chapel. Primitive Methodist Chapel. "Labour
in Vain" Inn (Wm. Smithson). "Loggerheads" Inn
(F. West). "Rose and Crown" Inn (B. Tarry).

[*The curtain rises on the Grange kitchen in the village
of Pantacks, one January morning. The Grange is one
of the very old farmhouses, and its kitchen would gladden
the eyes of an American. The open fireplace, with seats
inside the chimney, has a peat fire on its hearthstone
which burns with a thick blue fragrant smoke. Inside
and around the chimney are various hooks, chains, and
racks for hanging kettles and pots, smoking bacon, etc. ;
and there is a spit, long unused, but still carefully
cleaned. On the mantelpiece is a collection of brass
candlesticks of various sizes and shapes, an oval tobacco
box, and two snuffers complete with trays. The oak
beams that support the ceiling are dark with the smoke of
generations, and from them hang flitches of bacon, hams,
bladders of lard, two muskets, and a rifle. The wall-
paper, of floral design, has fortunately toned down into
keeping with the fine specimen of a grandfather clock and
the copper warming-pans. The floor is of stone slabs*

*without any covering. The furniture is of black oak, and if Pantacks were not down in the Gulland Marshes, the Elmitts would, before now, have learned its value. The table in the centre, the arm-chair, and two small chairs beside it, and four others around the walls, together with the beautiful dresser, would draw a tempting offer.*

*The fireplace is in the centre of the back wall, and has on each side a casement window with leaded panes and deep window-seats. There is a door to the farmyard in the left wall, and beside it another door opens into what the Elmitts call their " second kitchen," where all the cooking is done. Between these doors hangs a whole range of polished metal dish-covers.*

*Sarah Tinsley is closing the door of a cupboard in the right-hand corner. She is an elderly woman, and has been at the Grange since she was a girl of fourteen. When Mrs. Elmitt died, Sarah became housekeeper as well as cook and general servant. A tiny woman, with scanty white hair, bright blue eyes, and cheeks like rich wrinkled pippins, she is restless, energetic, sharp-voiced, and altogether birdlike. She comes forward with a bottle of sherry, which she places on a tray on the dresser, together with three wine-glasses and a biscuit barrel. Whilst she is doing this, Tom Bones, the old farm foreman, comes in from the yard. Five feet high, and nearly as broad, with a rim of white whisker meeting his stubble hair, a waddling gait, and a wrinkled, leathery skin, Tom looks exactly like one of the farm animals. He wears dirty boots and leggings, a discoloured smock, and an indescribable hat.*]

*Bones.* I've took some of your hot water, missis, for Brutus.

*Sarah.* Your Jack said he wasn't very grand last night. What's the matter with him?

*Bones.* Colic, I reckon. Pedigree bulls has tender stomachs. It was a queer thing, him being took ill the very day of the poor Mester's funeral, wasn't it ? He thought the world of that old bull !

*Sarah*. No wonder ! Look what he paid Mester Dane for him.

*Bones*. He's worth double that to-day. A wonderful bull ! When I fetched him from Fletton, Albert Cook said he was the most promising youngster as they'd ever bred. I wonder who's going to have him. Was there a will ?

*Sarah* [*looking round apprehensively*]. I'm afraid not. Mester Smithson's coming across directly to talk to the two boys, and then we shall know how things stand.

*Bones*. I hope to goodness there *is* a will ! If there ain't, they say as the eldest takes all.

*Sarah*. That would be very unfair to Mester James.

*Bones* [*dubiously*]. Mester Charles is giving orders all round as if he owned everything. You don't think he does, do you ?

*Sarah*. I don't feel very easy about it, but we shall know soon. Have you seen Mester James this morning ?

*Bones*. He's been round as usual, but he hardly spoke a word.

*Sarah*. He's feeling the Mester's death very much.

*Bones*. I know which I'd sooner have in the old gentleman's place. [SARAH *puts her finger to her lips*.] I don't care if anybody *does* hear ;—drinking and gambling and carrying on. If Mester Charles is boss, it'll be a sad day for us all.

*Sarah*. It will indeed ! But we must hope for the best. I suppose, anyhow, you'll have to flit from the Dovecote into one of the cottages.

*Bones* [*gloomily*]. There's nothing but changes. Only t'other day Squire Rupert died, as had been at the Manor ever since I was a lad ; and now our good old Mester's gone. Squire Christopher's turning everything upside down with his new-fangled ideas, till nobody knows if they're standing on their heads or their heels.

*Sarah.* We *shall* know which, if there isn't a will : we shall be on our heels—out in the road—for all our years of service.

*Bones.* Who'd look after the old bull if I was gone, I don't know.

*Sarah.* And me, what nursed him from the very first ! But he's never cared for nobody but himself, hasn't Mester Charles.

*Bones.* The poor Mester sent for me only last Monday, as ever was. Bones, he says, you must take care of Brutus when I'm gone. You understand him, he says ; and I told him I would as long as I had breath in my body.

*Sarah.* What was the good of telling you that, if he didn't leave Brutus to Mester James ?

*Bones.* You should have reminded him to make a will.

*Sarah.* That was likely, wasn't it ? Our Mester wasn't one as you could say things to—like you can to Mester James.

[*The yard door opens and* JAMES ELMITT *enters. He is a tall, thin fellow of four-and-twenty, who stoops slightly ; dressed in his Sunday blacks.*

*James.* How's Brutus now, Tom ?

*Bones.* We've just been fomenting of him, Mester James, and going to give him another directly.

*James.* If he isn't better by dinner, we'll wire to Fletton for Enderby Hicks. It's unfortunate being Barkston Show to-morrow.

*Bones.* I know he'd a took the first prize.

*James* [*sitting down in the ingle-nook and lighting a cigarette*]. Well, he can't go, and that's certain ! But it's no good worrying about it, Tom ; there'll be another day.

*Bones.* I'll go and have another look at him. [*Shak-*

*ing his head mournfully*] I'm sure he'd a took the first prize. [*He waddles toward the yard door.*

*Sarah.* We shall be wanting some more turf, Mester James. We must keep a good fire up this cold weather.

*James.* We shan't run short of that, shall we, Tom ?

*Bones.* We took enough out of the Fen last summer to keep us going for three winters. [*Exit.*

*Sarah* [*going nearer to* JAMES]. Did you find a will ?

*James* [*shaking his head slowly*]. We've hunted everywhere, high and low ; but I'm afraid father left it too late.

*Sarah.* That wasn't like the poor dear Mester.

*James.* I can't understand it at all, Sarah. When he told me that " things would be all right," I never gave it another thought.

*Sarah.* What about Lawyer White ? Your father always went to him.

*James.* If he'd had a will, we should have heard from him before now.

*Sarah* [*lowering her voice*]. You don't think it's been done away with ?

[JAMES *shakes his head, and* SARAH *is about to say something further, when she hears steps coming down the stone corridor, and taking from the table the cloth with which she had dusted the wine-glasses, retires into her own kitchen. As she closes the door,* CHARLES ELMITT *enters on the right, and crosses to the yard door, whistling as he goes. He sees* JAMES *in the ingle-nook and stops.*

[*The eldest son of the dead farmer is inclined to stoutness, although not much older than his brother, and if it were not for his out-of-door life would already begin to look bloated. His clothes have been cut by Noel Andrews—the Bly sporting tailor—and his leggings are highly polished.*

*Charles* [*in a jeering voice, giving* JAMES *a sharp poke with his riding whip*]. Now then, wake up, sloomy sides ; you're always dreaming.

*James* [*staring into the fire*]. I was thinking of the poor old Governor.

*Charles* [*leaning against the fireplace, opposite* JAMES]. Your thinking won't bring him back to life.

*James.* He was a good father to us, Charles.

*Charles* [*sneering*]. You'll find it more important to be a good brother to me now.

*James* [*aroused by this, and coming out of the inglenook*]. Oh, why should I ?

*Charles.* The sooner you realize *that* the better for you.

*James.* I don't know why you're talking like this. Father said he'd provided for me.

*Charles.* I'll tell you once for all what he did, and then you'll know. The dividing of the property is left entirely in my hands, as the eldest. Those were the old man's very words.

*James.* But he told me I was provided for.

*Charles.* So you are ! He left it to me to provide for you, so let's have no nonsense.

*James.* We'll see what Uncle William says.

*Charles* [*seeing the sherry, and helping himself*]. Uncle William ! He always wants to shove his nose into everything. He said he was coming over this morning to talk to us, and I shall listen to what he says—but that's all !

*James.* I can't understand it.

*Charles.* Perhaps you expected to be left in one of the farms. [*Laughing*] I'm master now, and I can tell you things are going to be very different. We've been cluttered up long enough with a lot of doddering old fools like Bones and Casswell.

*James* [*horrified*]. You won't sack Bones ! Father said there wasn't a more trusty man with stock this side the Gulland.  He's worked here all his life.

*Charles.* Time he had a change, then. The old man pleased himself, and I'm going to do the same.

*James.* Father promised Bones he shouldn't be pushed on one side : I heard him.

*Charles.* I've nothing whatever to do with other folk's promises. If Bones was to square himself up and be civil, I might keep him.

*James.* He's too old to alter now. But what's his manners amount to ?

*Charles.* A good deal too much for me. I'm blowed if the men aren't getting to be as good as the masters nowadays. I don't know as they aren't better off than us.

*James.* You wouldn't change places, though.

*Charles* [*filling his pipe*]. I've seen our chaps that close together on a stack that they couldn't move their forks for fear of brogging one another. But I'll alter that !

*James.* They may be slow, but they're steady. Don't be too sharp, Charles.

*Charles.* And don't you be so fauce,* Jimmy. You'll have as much as you can manage to keep your own place, without sticking up for that lazy gang.

[*The conversation ceases on the appearance of* SARAH *from her kitchen. She hesitates which to address, and looks tactfully between them as she speaks.*

*Sarah.* There's a man by the name of Patchett from Mester Titus Ambrose's wants to know where you want the threshing machine putting.

*Charles* [*authoritatively*]. Go and arrange it with him, Jimmy. We shall want him here first.

[JAMES *goes out, and* CHARLES *takes another glass of sherry.* SARAH *is about to protest, but thinks better of it.* CHARLES *seats himself in the armchair, which he pushes back from the table.*

* *Fauce* (Lincolnshire), impertinent, presumptuous : nearly always addressed to children.

*Sarah.* Where's the black tie you wore at the funeral, Mester Charles?

*Charles.* I've something better to do than sit and mope in blacks. [*Stretching his legs out luxuriously*] A rare farmer Jimmy would make! A foreman's all he's fit for, and that's what he's going to be. I've been planning things out a bit this morning, Sarah.

*Sarah* [*non-committally*]. Oh!

*Charles.* I can do as I like now everything belongs to me; and one of the first things is, I'm going to be married right away!

*Sarah.* Not directly after the funeral, surely?

*Charles.* I shall put Jimmy in the Dovecote farm-house instead of Bones, and, if he likes, you can keep house for him.

*Sarah.* Will the Squire let you keep both farms? Your father said he was the only farmer on any estate round here as was allowed to have two such houses; and that was only on account of his taking the Dovecote over in the bad times, when nobody else would have it.

*Charles.* I know how to manage the Squire. I'm going to straighten things up all round, and shan't let any silly old ideas stand in *my* way, any more than he's done. That yew's coming down.

*Sarah.* Mester Charles, you can't do that! The old tree was here in your great-grandfather's time.

*Charles.* I don't care a damn about that! It shades the front windows, and it's coming down now —right away! You'll hear it directly.

[*Flabbergasted by this piece of news,* SARAH *goes through the door on the right to see for herself what is happening in the front garden.* CHARLES *rises and pours himself out a third glassful of sherry as* BONES *enters from the yard.*

*Bones* [*bluntly*]. What's this our Jack tells me about the old bull being got ready to go to the Show?

*Charles* [*tossing off the sherry*]. Say *Sir*, when you speak to me.

*Bones.* What for ?

*Charles.* Because I'm master.

*Bones.* Oh ! . . . all right !

*Charles* [*sitting down and trying to look like his father used to*]. Now then, what is it you want ?

*Bones.* What's this our Jack tells me about the old bull being got ready to go to the Show ?

*Charles.* Haven't I just told you to say *Sir*, when you speak to me ?

*Bones.* He's not fit to go to no Shows.

*Charles.* That's for me to say.

*Bones.* Mester James has had a look at him, and says he can't go.

*Charles* [*furiously*]. What the devil is it to do with you or him ? I say he *is* going.

*Bones.* You must be crazed.

*Charles* [*recovering himself*]. I've told you what to do, and that's plenty.

*Bones.* That's all very well, but you don't know nothing about *bulls*. I was tending to 'em before you was ever thought of.

*Charles.* Yes, you're old-fashioned enough.

*Bones.* You won't find many as knows more about stock than me, and chance the ducks ! Old Mester had sense enough to let me alone. Bones, he says to me many a time, Bones, you might almost have been a bull yourself. Of course, you can cut old Brutus up and make soup of him, but if you want to do yourself any good you must hearken to me.

*Charles.* And if you want to do *yourself* any good you'll do what I tell you.

[*A dull crash is heard, and the kitchen shakes slightly.*

*Bones.* What's yon ?

[*Before* CHARLES *can answer,* SARAH *comes in from the corridor, looking very upset.*

*Sarah.* It's down! It's down!

*Charles.* Of course it's down!

*Sarah.* You mark my words, Mester Charles, cutting that old yew down'll bring you no luck.

*Bones.* You don't mean to say——

*Charles* [*violently*]. You'd better both of you understand right away that I'm mester here now. You're too fond of forgetting your places. I don't want any back talk from *servants*, and I'm not going to have it.

*Sarah* [*losing control*]. What do you know about servants; trying to lord it over everybody? And me what nursed you as a baby—a nasty-tempered one you was and all.

*Charles* [*trying hard to look dignified*]. That's enough, Sarah.

*Sarah* [*with immense scorn*]. Sitting there, trying to look like your father! It isn't five minutes since you was running about in petticoats and squalling for me to pick you up.

*Charles* [*losing all control*]. Get out of this kitchen. I'll sack you!

*Together* {

  *Sarah.* Sack me! What's been here since I was fourteen! We'll see what Mester Smithson says to that!

  *Bones.* Steady on, Mester Charles, steady on! You can't run at things a-that-ow!

  *Charles* [*shouting at the top of his voice to try and drown them*]. Shut up! Clear out! Shut up!

}

[*At the height of the tumult the yard door opens and* WILLIAM SMITHSON *comes in, followed by* JAMES. UNCLE WILLIAM, *the landlord of the " Labour in Vain " Inn, is also an auctioneer and valuer, and looks entirely prosperous. He is dressed in a blue suit of good cloth, and has mutton-chop whiskers, grey hair, and a com-*

*fortable paunch. There is a mourning-band round his left arm, and another round his wide-brimmed bowler. He takes instant command of the situation, speaking in a powerful bass voice.*

*Uncle William.* Hallo! Hallo! What's all this noise about?

*Sarah.* The new mester's sacking everybody.

*Charles.* I will, if they don't shut up.

*Uncle William* [*putting his hand up for order, and seating himself in the arm-chair at the table, whilst the others cluster round him*]. Now tell me all about it.

[*This request is immediately fatal.*

*Together*

*Charles.* I'm master here, aren't I? What I say is law, and the sooner everybody gets settled down to that, the better.

*Sarah.* He's no business to go on so soft, trying to turn me out into the street, what's been here since I was fourteen.

*Bones.* I'm all for bulls, I am, but if you don't treat 'em fair, what can you expect but trouble.

*James* [*to* SARAH]. Now, now, Sarah, wait a minute! [*To* BONES] Be quiet, Tom!

*Uncle William* [*banging his fist on the table and uttering a terrific roar*]. NO! NO! NO! NO! NO! [UNCLE WILLIAM'S *bellow is so terrible that it brings them all to a standstill. More cautious this time, he points his finger at* CHARLES, *and says*] Now, Charles, you first.

*Charles.* I'm master here, and I'll have no cheek from nobody.

*Sarah.* You started it, talking about getting rid of Mester James and me and Tom, and going and chopping the old yew down.

*Charles.* I shall do just what I like. I'm master.

*Uncle William.* How do you know you're master?

*Bones.* Ay!

*Sarah.* Ah!

*Charles.* I know right enough. There's no will, and everything's mine.

*James.* It's a poor lookout for me, then, uncle.

*Uncle William.* That's what I've come to talk about.

*Charles* [*arrogantly*]. You can talk, all of you, but to ease your minds I'll tell you that father said he was leaving the dividing of the property in *my* hands as the eldest. [*All look aghast, except* UNCLE WILLIAM.] So that's all there is about it!

*Uncle William.* Have you done, Charles?

*Charles.* Yes, I have.

*Uncle William.* Then I'll begin. [*Unbuttoning his coat, he draws a long, sealed envelope from an inner pocket.*] I'll now read your father's will.

*Charles.* What's that?

*James.* I felt sure there was one.

[BONES *and* SARAH *nudge each other.*

*Charles.* How came you to have it—all this time?

*Uncle William.* I am executor. [*He pauses to let this sink in.*] Your father gave me this will just before Christmas, when he began to feel he wasn't going to get better, and he charged me to say nothing about it to any one until after the funeral. [*He glances at* CHARLES.] He said he didn't want to have any wrangling over his dead body.

*Charles.* Well! It makes no difference. I've told you what's in it.

[*He looks at* BONES *and* SARAH, *and indicates by a jerk of his head that they are both to leave. They turn to go.*

*Uncle William.* No! You both stop here.

*Charles.* I'm not going to have servants listening to my private affairs.

*Uncle William* [*blandly*]. They're mentioned in the will.

*Charles* [*staggered*]. Oh!... But they needn't hear it all.

*Uncle William.* They've as much right to hear it all as you have.

*Charles* [*sulkily*]. Let's have it then.

*Uncle William.* All in good time. [*He takes his glasses out of their case and puts them on.*] When you're my age and weight, my lad, you won't hurry. [*He breaks open the seal, draws the will out of its envelope, and begins to read.*] "This is the Will of me, Ernest Elmitt, farmer, of Pantacks. Squire Harbord has been kind enough to say that my sons may carry on the two farms, so I leave all my property to be divided by my eldest son, Charles, according to the instructions below. There is the live and dead stock and implements for 386 acres at the Grange Farm, and the live and dead stock and implements for 293 acres at the Dovecote Farm, the money at the Old County Bank at Bly, the furniture at the Grange, and anything else that may belong to me at my death. Lastly, my pedigree bull, Brutus, who will make anybody's fortune if taken care of. [BONES *nods his head so violently that* SARAH *has to restrain him.*] Whichever of my sons takes the Dovecote shall pay to my faithful foreman, Tom Bones, the sum of One hundred pounds whenever he leaves, and whichever takes the Grange shall do the same for my faithful servant, Sarah Tinsley. But I hope neither of them will go as long as they live. [JAMES *quietly pats* SARAH *on the back.*] All my property mentioned above is to be divided by my son Charles into two lists, and—[UNCLE WILLIAM *pauses dramatically*] and my son James shall have the first pick."

*Charles.* I don't believe a word of it. Father told me different. He said I was to divide things up just as I liked.

*Uncle William.* So you do ! It says so, doesn't it ?

*Charles* [*overtaxed*]. Oh ! . . . That's all right, then.

*Uncle William.* Let me finish. " These lists shall

be signed by both my sons and handed to William Smithson, my wife's brother. I have appointed William to be my Executor, and leave to him the sum of Twenty-five pounds and Grandfather Abraham's brass tobacco-box. Signed at Bly in the presence of Arthur Dickinson, lawyer's clerk, and Samuel Lupton, lawyer's clerk.—ERNEST ELMITT."

*Charles.* That will was never drawn by a lawyer, and I don't believe it will hold water. I'm the eldest son, and I know what father told me.

*Uncle William.* Your father wrote that will himself, Charles, and took it to Lawyer White for him to look it over. Lawyer White, of course, wanted to put it in long legal words, but your father wouldn't have that. He said he wanted it to be his own words in his own writing, so as there could be no wrangling about what he meant. I'll pay you your proper fee, he says to Lawyer White, for making my will, but I don't want it altered unless there's anything in it as isn't water-tight. Lawyer White conned it over and owned—at the finish—as it was a good will, and it wouldn't profit any one to try and upset it.

*Bones.* You take Brutus, Mester James.

*Charles* [*venting his rage on* BONES]. Clear out ! I'll sack you !

*Uncle William.* So you're taking the Dovecote, are you ?

*Charles.* What do you mean ?

*Uncle William.* Bones goes with the Dovecote. If you take that, you can sack him all right, so long as you pay him his hundred pounds.

*Sarah.* So you'd no right to have that old yew cut down, after all !

*Charles* [*in a fighting rage*]. Who asked you to speak, you vixen ?

*Sarah.* You're not my mester, thank goodness !

*Charles.* I *am* master, and I'll sack you as well.

*Uncle William.* Then it's the Grange you're going

to have, is it ? [CHARLES *looks puzzled.*] You can't very well sack Sarah unless you take the Grange.

*Sarah.* And give me my hundred pounds.

[CHARLES *by this time is completely befogged ; and looks it. The others laugh at his predicament.*

*Charles.* It's a lot of rot, and I'm damned if I'm going to stand it. You can all go——

*Uncle William* [*interrupting him sharply*]. That's enough, Charles ; I won't have it.

*Charles.* Oh, won't you ?

*Uncle William.* No, I won't ! *I'm* master here at present.

*Charles.* Oh no, you're not !

*Uncle William.* Yes, I am. I'm executor, and I'm going to execute without fear or favour ; so let's get to business. You make your two lists out.

[JAMES *has whispered in* SARAH'S *ear, and she now produces a packet of writing paper, a pen, and a bottle of ink, which she puts on the table.*

*Charles* [*sulkily*]. All right, then !

*Sarah.* You won't want us any more, Mester Smithson, shall you ?

*Uncle William.* No, thank you, Sarah. [*He glances at the dresser, and* SARAH, *seeing the look, gives an exclamation of dismay, and fetches the tray of refreshments from the dresser.*] Get out two more glasses, Sarah.

[*Whilst* SARAH *fetches these,* JAMES *reaches down the oval tobacco-box from the mantelpiece, and gives it to* UNCLE WILLIAM, *who looks at it affectionately and drops it in his coat pocket. He then pours sherry into the five glasses, and they all drink.* SARAH *then goes out.*

*Charles* [*to* BONES, *who is following* SARAH]. Just hang about a few minutes, Bones : I may want to know something about the stock.

[BONES *nods shortly, and goes out, muttering to himself about the old bull wanting him.*

*Uncle William* [*to* CHARLES, *who is sitting on the left of the table, sucking the end of his pen*]. Come along, Charles. We're waiting.

*Charles.* How can I, with you both staring at me like stuck rats ! [*He scratches his head, licks the pen nib, writes something on one of the two sheets of paper in front of him ; then looks up.*] You wouldn't want the biggest house to live in, Jimmy. [JAMES *says nothing to this.*] If the two farms were the same size, it would be easy. [*Irritably*] Say something, can't you ?

*James.* There's nothing for me to say. You make your lists out, and I'll take which I want.

*Uncle William* [*taking more sherry*]. That's it. Make the lists out, Charles.

> [CHARLES *scratches his head again, gives the pen another dip in the ink, then stares hopelessly at the paper. As this doesn't get him any further, he turns in his chair and shouts* "BONES." BONES *comes in unwillingly, still muttering about the bull.*

*Charles.* How many sheep are there in the far field by Isaac Cheetham's ?

*Bones.* There's 87 in the grass field, and 93 in the fallows, but one of them died yesterday, and I aren't sure but what we shan't lose another before the day's done. That's the worst of sheep ! Give me a good bull, I say.

> [CHARLES *writes, whilst* BONES *speaks in a hoarse whisper to* JAMES.

*Bones.* You pick the old bull, Mester James.

*James* [*hushing him*]. We'll see, Tom.

*Bones* [*refusing to be hushed*]. I'm all for bulls, I am.

*Charles.* Which of the farms does that new Yankee binder go with ?

*Bones.* Sometimes one, and sometimes t'other.

*Charles.* Yes, but which of 'em does it *belong* to ?

*Bones.* This year we had her first at the Grange ;

last year she was first at the Dovecote, and the year afore that we lent her first to George Baldock.

*Charles* [*throwing down his pen and rising*]. How the devil can I put everything down on two lists! [*He stares angrily at the others ; then reseats himself, takes two fresh sheets of paper, and scribbles hastily on the top of each.*] That's it. Here you are, Jimmy! [*He offers one of the papers to* JAMES, *who takes it.*] I stop here in the Grange and keep Brutus, while you go to the Dovecote.

*Uncle William.* Have you put that on your lists, Charles ? [CHARLES *nods.*] Then let's have a look at them. [JAMES *hands his to* UNCLE WILLIAM *promptly, and* CHARLES *does the same reluctantly.* UNCLE WILLIAM *examines the lists in turn, reading out, "The Dovecote Farm and all that goes with it ;" and "The Grange Farm and all that goes with it, including the pedigree bull, Brutus."*] That's your two lists, is it ?

*Charles.* Yes!

*Uncle William.* Very well, then : James, you have the first pick.

*Charles* [*hastily*]. Oh no, he doesn't! He takes what I offer him.

*Uncle William* [*firmly*]. James has the first pick.

*Charles.* He isn't going to have the Grange, nor yet Brutus.

*Uncle William.* He is, if he picks them.

*Charles.* Then I shall put Brutus on the Dovecote list.

*James* [*promptly*]. Then I can pick the Dovecote.

*Charles* [*snatching up both lists*]. You won't!

*Uncle William.* That's what the will says, Charles —he has the first pick.

*Bones* [*unable to restrain himself*]. Stick to the old bull, Mester James, and he'll stick to you. He's a good 'un.

*Sarah* [*who is now standing in the doorway, taking a step forward and pulling at* BONES'S *smock*]. Be quiet!

*Bones.* I'm all for bulls, I am.

*Uncle William* [*rapping on the table*]. This won't do! Charles, you must offer James the choice, according to the will, and then abide by it.

*Charles* [*as the full horror of the situation dawns upon him*]. Do you mean to say that, however I draw the lists up, Jimmy can pick which he likes?

*Uncle William.* That's what the will says.

*Charles.* Well, I'm damned!

[*He sits down again, and presently begins to make two fresh lists.*

*Bones.* Don't you let old Brutus go, Mester James. [SARAH *tries to keep him quiet.*] But it's the old bull.

*Sarah.* It's the old goat, I think—you and your whiskers!

*Bones.* He's worth his weight in gold. You don't know that old bull, or you'd talk different.

[*A voice is heard outside, calling urgently for "Mester Bones."* TOM, *hearing this, turns and hurries out into the yard.*

*Charles* [*putting down his pen with an air of relief*]. There you are! I've done 'em!

*Uncle William.* And are you prepared to abide by them?

*Charles.* Yes!

*Uncle William.* Then, James, you look at them carefully and make your choice.

[JAMES *leans over* CHARLES'S *shoulder to look at the two lists.* CHARLES'S *hand is resting casually on the bottom of one of the sheets, and when* JAMES *tries to get it away,* CHARLES *holds it down.*

*James.* I want to see what's at the bottom of that.

*Uncle William* [*very sharply*]. Now then, Charles.

*James* [*taking it up as* CHARLES *releases it*]. I thought so! He was hiding Brutus. I'll have this list.

*Charles* [*snatching it from him*]. Oh no, you won't!

*Uncle William* [*speaking in his sternest and most*

*formidable manner*]. Charles, you're behaving like a child, and I'm not going to stop here all the morning to be made a fool of. Do you think we're all idiots?

*Charles* [*in despair*]. I can't make any more lists out. Jimmy, you take the Grange, and I'll take the Dovecote and Brutus. That's as fair as I can do.

*James.* Well—that's the fairest offer we've had yet.

*Uncle William.* Let's see it down on paper.

[CHARLES *writes again on two fresh sheets and hands them to* JAMES.

*James.* Yes, I think that's about fair. [*He considers for a moment; then turns to* UNCLE WILLIAM.] I'll stop here in the Grange.

*Charles.* And I go to the Dovecote and take Brutus.

*Uncle William.* I suppose you do know, James, that Colishaw Bell offered your father six hundred and seventy guineas for Brutus, at Holt Foal Fair last September?

*James.* I was there with father—but I'd like to stop in the old home.

*Uncle William.* Very well, then. Are you both agreed on that?

*James.* Yes, uncle. [CHARLES *nods.*

*Uncle William.* Well . . . I don't think you could have done it much evener, taking everything all round. Now you must both sign your names underneath these lists, and Sarah and I'll witness the signatures. [*All sign.* UNCLE WILLIAM *folds up the two lists and puts them with the will into the envelope.*] Now I must turn it all over to Lawyer White.

*James* [*to* SARAH]. Won't poor old Tom be disappointed?

*Sarah.* I'm very thankful as you've got the old home, Mester James.

*Uncle William.* I must get off to Bly——

[*The door bursts open and* BONES *waddles in from the yard at top speed, the picture of consternation.*

*Bones.* The old bull, the old bull ! Oh dear ! Oh dear ! The old bull !

*All.* What ? What's the matter ? What is it ?

*Bones.* When I went out to him, he just raised one horn in the air, as much as to say good-bye, then shut his eyes. Now he lays yonder with his tail straight out, and never a breath in his body. I never ought to have left him. Oh dear ! Oh dear ! What would the old Mester have said ?

*Charles.* That alters everything. Give me the lists back.                   [*He tries to snatch the envelope.*

*Uncle William* [*holding him off, and tucking the envelope away into his inner pocket*]. Oh no, my boy ! [*He buttons up his coat.*] When you'd signed the lists, you both stood at your own risk. You can't change any more.

*Sarah.* Cutting down that old yew hasn't brought you any luck, Mester Charles.

*Bones* [*speaking sadly and slowly*]. There wasn't another bull like him nowhere. We shall never see his likes again.

CURTAIN

# THE OLD BULL.

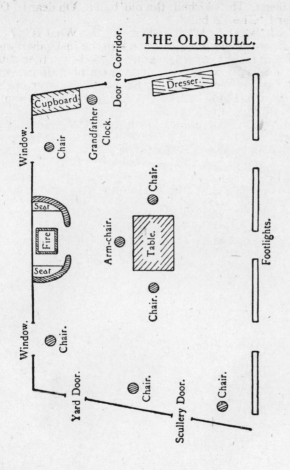

# THE LITTLE MAN

## A FARCICAL MORALITY

### IN THREE SCENES

### BY JOHN GALSWORTHY

# CHARACTERS

| | |
|---|---|
| THE LITTLE MAN. | THE MOTHER. |
| THE AMERICAN. | THE BABY. |
| THE ENGLISHMAN. | THE WAITER. |
| THE ENGLISHWOMAN. | THE STATION OFFICIAL. |
| THE GERMAN. | THE POLICEMAN. |
| THE DUTCH BOY. | THE PORTER. |

# THE LITTLE MAN

## SCENE I

*Afternoon, on the departure platform of an Austrian railway station. At several little tables outside the buffet persons are taking refreshment, served by a pale young waiter. On a seat against the wall of the buffet a woman of lowly station is sitting beside two large bundles, on one of which she has placed her baby, swathed in a black shawl.*

*Waiter [approaching a table whereat sit an English traveller and his wife].* Two coffee ?

*Englishman [paying].* Thanks. [*To his wife, in an Oxford voice*] Sugar ?

*Englishwoman [in a Cambridge voice].* One.

*American Traveller [with field-glasses and a pocket camera—from another table.]* Waiter, I'd like to have you get my eggs. I've been sitting here quite a while.

*Waiter.* Yes, sare.

*German Traveller.* Kellner, bezahlen ! [*His voice is, like his moustache, stiff and brushed up at the ends. His figure also is stiff and his hair a little grey ; clearly once, if not now, a colonel.*]

*Waiter.* Komm' gleich !

> [*The* BABY *on the bundle wails. The* MOTHER *takes it up to soothe it. A young, red-cheeked Dutchman at the fourth table stops eating and laughs.*

119

*American.* My eggs ! Get a wiggle on you !

*Waiter.* Yes, sare.                    [*He rapidly recedes.*

[*A* LITTLE MAN *in a soft hat is seen to the right of tables. He stands a moment looking after the hurrying waiter, then seats himself at the fifth table.*

*Englishman* [*looking at his watch*]. Ten minutes more.

*Englishwoman.* Bother !

*American* [*addressing them*]. 'Pears as if they'd a prejudice against eggs here, anyway.

[*The* ENGLISH *look at him, but do not speak.*

*German* [*in creditable English*]. In these places man can get nothing.

[*The* WAITER *comes flying back with a compote for the* DUTCH YOUTH, *who pays.*

*German.* Kellner, bezahlen !

*Waiter.* Eine Krone sechzig.    [*The* GERMAN *pays.*

*American* [*rising, and taking out his watch—blandly*]. See here. If I don't get my eggs before this watch ticks twenty, there'll be another waiter in heaven.

*Waiter* [*flying*]. Komm' gleich !

*American* [*seeking sympathy*]. I'm gettin' kind of mad !

[*The* ENGLISHMAN *halves his newspaper and hands the advertisement half to his wife. The* BABY *wails. The* MOTHER *rocks it. The* DUTCH YOUTH *stops eating and laughs. The* GERMAN *lights a cigarette. The* LITTLE MAN *sits motionless, nursing his hat. The* WAITER *comes flying back with the eggs and places them before the* AMERICAN.

*American* [*putting away his watch*]. Good ! I don't like trouble. How much ?

[*He pays and eats. The* WAITER *stands a moment at the edge of the platform and passes his hand across his brow. The* LITTLE MAN *eyes him and speaks gruffly.*

*Little Man.* Herr Ober ! [*The* WAITER *turns.*]
Might I have a glass of beer ?

*Waiter.* Yes, sare.

*Little Man.* Thank you very much.

[*The* WAITER *goes.*

*American* [*pausing in the deglutition of his eggs—
affably*]. Pardon me, sir ; I'd like to have you tell me
why you called that little bit of a feller " Herr Ober."
Reckon you would know what that means ?  Mr.
Head Waiter.

*Little Man.* Yes, yes.

*American.* I smile.

*Little Man.* Oughtn't I to call him that ?

*German* [*abruptly*]. Nein—Kellner.

*American.* Why, yes !  Just " waiter."

[*The* ENGLISHWOMAN *looks round her paper for a
second. The* DUTCH YOUTH *stops eating and
laughs. The* LITTLE MAN *gazes from face to
face and nurses his hat.*

*Little Man.* I didn't want to hurt his feelings.

*German.* Gott !

*American.* In my country we're very democratic—
but that's quite a proposition.

*Englishman* [*handling coffee-pot, to his wife*]. More ?

*Englishwoman.* No, thanks.

*German* [*abruptly*]. These fellows—if you treat them
in this manner, at once they take liberties.  You see,
you will not get your beer.

[*As he speaks the* WAITER *returns, bringing the*
LITTLE MAN'S *beer, then retires.*

*American.* That 'pears to be one up to democracy.
[*To the* LITTLE MAN] I judge you go in for brotherhood ?

*Little Man* [*startled*]. Oh no !

*American.* I take considerable stock in Leo Tolstoi
myself.  Grand man—grand-souled apparatus.  But
I guess you've got to pinch those waiters some to make
'em skip. [*To the* ENGLISH, *who have carelessly looked*

*his way for a moment*] You'll appreciate that, the way he acted about my eggs.

[*The* ENGLISH *make faint motions with their chins and avert their eyes.*

[*To the* WAITER, *who is standing at the door of the buffet*] Waiter! Flash of beer—jump, now!

*Waiter.* Komm' gleich!

*German.* Cigarren!

*Waiter.* Scöhn!                    [*He disappears.*

*American* [*affably—to the* LITTLE MAN]. Now, if I don't get that flash of beer quicker'n you got yours, I shall admire.

*German* [*abruptly*]. Tolstoi is nothing—nichts! No good! Ha?

*American* [*relishing the approach of argument*]. Well, that is a matter of temperament. Now, I'm all for equality. See that poor woman there—very humble woman—there she sits among us with her baby. Perhaps you'd like to locate her somewhere else?

*German* [*shrugging*]. Tolstoi is sentimentalisch. Nietzsche is the true philosopher, the only one.

*American.* Well, that's quite in the prospectus—very stimulating party—old Nietch—virgin mind. But give me Leo! [*He turns to the red-cheeked* YOUTH] What do you opine, sir? I guess by your labels you'll be Dutch. Do they read Tolstoi in your country?

                    [*The* DUTCH YOUTH *laughs.*

*American.* That is a very luminous answer.

*German.* Tolstoi is nothing. Man should himself express. He must push—he must be strong.

*American.* That is so. In America we believe in virility; we like a man to expand. But we believe in brotherhood too. We draw the line at niggers; but we aspire. Social barriers and distinctions we've not much use for.

*Englishman.* Do you feel a draught?

*Englishwoman* [*with a shiver of her shoulder toward the* AMERICAN]. I do—rather.

*German.* Wait ! You are a young people.

*American.* That is so ; there are no flies on us. [*To the* LITTLE MAN, *who has been gazing eagerly from face to face*] Say ! I'd like to have you give us your sentiments in relation to the duty of man.

> [*The* LITTLE MAN *fidgets, and is about to open his mouth.*

*American.* For example—is it your opinion that we should kill off the weak and diseased, and all that can't jump around ?

*German* [*nodding*]. Ja, ja ! That is coming.

*Little Man* [*looking from face to face*]. They might be me.                    [*The* DUTCH YOUTH *laughs.*

*American* [*reproving him with a look*]. That's true humility. 'Tisn't grammar. Now, here's a proposition that brings it nearer the bone : Would you step out of your way to help them when it was liable to bring you trouble ?

*German.* Nein, nein ! That is stupid.

*Little Man* [*eager but wistful*]. I'm afraid not. Of course one wants to—— There was St. Francis d'Assisi and St. Julien l'Hospitalier, and——

*American.* Very lofty dispositions. Guess they died of them. [*He rises.*] Shake hands, sir—my name is—— [*He hands a card.*] I am an ice-machine maker. [*He shakes the* LITTLE MAN's *hand.*] I like your sentiments—I feel kind of brotherly. [*Catching sight of the* WAITER *appearing in the doorway*] Waiter, where to h——ll is that flash of beer ?

*German.* Cigarren !

*Waiter.* Komm' gleich !                    [*He vanishes.*

*Englishman* [*consulting watch*]. Train's late.

*Englishwoman.* Really ! Nuisance !

> [*A station* POLICEMAN, *very square and uniformed, passes and repasses.*

*American* [*resuming his seat—to the* GERMAN]. Now, we don't have so much of that in America. Guess we feel more to trust in human nature.

*German.* Ah ! ha ! you will bresently find there is nothing in him but self.

*Little Man* [*wistfully*]. Don't you believe in human nature ?

*American.* Very stimulating question. [*He looks round for opinions.*]    [*The* DUTCH YOUTH *laughs.*

*Englishman* [*holding out his half of the paper to his wife*]. Swap !    [*His wife swaps.*

*German.* In human nature I believe so far as I can see him—no more.

*American.* Now that 'pears to me kind o' blasphemy. I believe in heroism. I opine there's not one of us settin' around here that's not a hero—give him the occasion.

*Little Man.* Oh ! Do you believe that ?

*American.* Well ! I judge a hero is just a person that'll help another at the expense of himself. Take that poor woman there. Well, now, she's a heroine, I guess. She would die for her baby any old time.

*German.* Animals will die for their babies. That is nothing.

*American.* I carry it further. I postulate we would all die for that baby if a locomotive was to trundle up right here and try to handle it. [*To the* GERMAN] I guess *you* don't know how good you are. [*As the* GERMAN *is twisting up the ends of his moustache—to the* ENGLISHWOMAN] I should like to have you express an opinion, ma'am.

*Englishwoman.* I beg your pardon.

*American.* The English are very humanitarian ; they have a very high sense of duty. So have the Germans, so have the Americans. [*To the* DUTCH YOUTH] I judge even in your little country they have that. This is an epoch of equality and high-toned ideals. [*To the* LITTLE MAN] What is *your* nationality, sir ?

*Little Man.* I'm afraid I'm nothing particular. My

father was half-English and half-American, and my mother half-German and half-Dutch.

*American.* My! That's a bit streaky, any old way. [*The* POLICEMAN *passes again.*] Now, I don't believe we've much use any more for those gentlemen in buttons. We've grown kind of mild—we don't think of self as we used to do.

> [*The* WAITER *has appeared in the doorway.*

*German* [*in a voice of thunder*]. Cigarren! Donnerwetter!

*American* [*shaking his fist at the vanishing* WAITER]. That flash of beer!

*Waiter.* Komm' gleich!

*American.* A little more, and he will join George Washington! I was about to remark when he intruded: In this year of grace 1913 the kingdom of Christ is quite a going concern. We are mighty near to universal brotherhood. The colonel here [*he indicates the* GERMAN] is a man of blood and iron, but give him an opportunity to be magnanimous, and he'll be right there. Oh, sir! yep!

> [*The* GERMAN, *with a profound mixture of pleasure and cynicism, brushes up the ends of his moustache.*

*Little Man.* I wonder. One wants to, but somehow—— [*He shakes his head.*]

*American.* You seem kind of skeery about that. You've had experience, maybe. I'm an optimist—I think we're bound to make the devil hum in the near future. I opine we shall occasion a good deal of trouble to that old party. There's about to be a holocaust of selfish interests. The colonel there with old-man Nietch—he won't know himself. There's going to be a very sacred opportunity.

> [*As he speaks, the voice of a* RAILWAY OFFICIAL *is heard in the distance calling out in German. It approaches, and the words become audible.*

*German* [*startled*]. Der Teufel ! [*He gets up, and seizes the bag beside him.*]

> [*The* STATION OFFICIAL *has appeared ; he stands for a moment casting his commands at the seated group. The* DUTCH YOUTH *also rises, and takes his coat and hat. The* OFFICIAL *turns on his heel and retires, still issuing directions.*

*Englishman.* What does he say ?

*German.* Our drain has come in, de oder platform ; only one minute we haf.    [*All have risen in a fluster.*

*American.* Now, that's very provoking.   I won't get that flash of beer.

> [*There is a general scurry to gather coats and hats and wraps, during which the lowly* WOMAN *is seen making desperate attempts to deal with her baby and the two large bundles. Quite defeated, she suddenly puts all down, wrings her hands, and cries out : " Herr Jesu !  Hilfe ! " The flying procession turn their heads at that strange cry.*

*American.* What's that ?   Help ?

> [*He continues to run.*

> [*The* LITTLE MAN *spins round, rushes back, picks up baby and bundle on which it was seated.*

*Little Man.* Come along, good woman, come along !

> [*The* WOMAN *picks up the other bundle and they run.*

> [*The* WAITER, *appearing in the doorway with the bottle of beer, watches with his tired smile.*

CURTAIN

# SCENE II

*A second-class compartment of a corridor carriage, in motion.  In it are seated the* ENGLISHMAN *and his* WIFE, *opposite each other at the corridor end, she with her face*

*to the engine, he with his back. Both are somewhat pro-*
*tected from the rest of the travellers by newspapers.*
*Next to her sits the* GERMAN, *and opposite him sits the*
AMERICAN ; *next the* AMERICAN *in one window corner*
*is seated the* DUTCH YOUTH ; *the other window corner is*
*taken by the* GERMAN'S *bag. The silence is only broken*
*by the slight rushing noise of the train's progression and*
*the crackling of the English newspapers.*

*American* [*turning to the* DUTCH YOUTH]. Guess I'd
like that window raised ; it's kind of chilly after that
old run they gave us.

> [*The* DUTCH YOUTH *laughs, and goes through the*
> *motions of raising the window. The* ENGLISH
> *regard the operation with uneasy irritation.*
> *The* GERMAN *opens his bag, which reposes on*
> *the corner seat next him, and takes out a book.*

*American.* The Germans are great readers. Very
stimulating practice. I read most anything myself !

> [*The* GERMAN *holds up the book so that the title*
> *may be read.*

*Don Quixote*—fine book. We Americans take considerable stock in old-man Quixote. Bit of a wild-cat
—but we don't laugh at him.

*German.* He is dead. Dead as a sheep. A good
thing, too.

*American.* In America we have still quite an
amount of chivalry.

*German.* Chivalry is nothing—sentimentalisch. In
modern days—no good. A man must push, he must
pull.

*American.* So you say. But I judge your form of
chivalry is sacrifice to the State. We allow more
freedom to the individual soul. Where there's something little and weak, we feel it kind of noble to give
up to it. That way we feel elevated.

> [*As he speaks there is seen in the corridor doorway*
> *the* LITTLE MAN, *with the* WOMAN'S BABY *still*

*on his arm and the bundle held in the other hand. He peers in anxiously. The* ENGLISH, *acutely conscious, try to dissociate themselves from his presence with their papers. The* DUTCH YOUTH *laughs.*

*German.* Ach ! So !

*American.* Dear me !

*Little Man.* Is there room ? I can't find a seat.

*American.* Why, yes ! There's a seat for one.

*Little Man* [*depositing bundle outside, and heaving* BABY]. May I ?

*American.* Come right in !

[*The* GERMAN *sulkily moves his bag. The* LITTLE MAN *comes in and seats himself gingerly.*

*American.* Where's the mother ?

*Little Man* [*ruefully*]. Afraid she got left behind.

[*The* DUTCH YOUTH *laughs. The* ENGLISH *unconsciously emerge from their newspapers.*

*American.* My ! That would appear to be quite a domestic incident.

[*The* ENGLISHMAN *suddenly utters a profound "Ha, ha !" and disappears behind his paper. And that paper and the one opposite are seen to shake, and little squirls and squeaks emerge.*

*German.* And you haf got her bundle, and her baby. Ha ! [*He cackles drily.*]

*American* [*gravely*]. I smile. I guess Providence has played it pretty low down on you. It's sure acted real mean.

[*The* BABY *wails, and the* LITTLE MAN *jigs it with a sort of gentle desperation, looking apologetically from face to face. His wistful glance renews the fire of merriment wherever it alights. The* AMERICAN *alone preserves a gravity which seems incapable of being broken.*

*American.* Maybe you'd better get off right smart and restore that baby. There's nothing can act madder than a mother.

*Little Man.* Poor thing, yes ! What she must be suffering !

[*A gale of laughter shakes the carriage. The* ENGLISH *for a moment drop their papers, the better to indulge. The* LITTLE MAN *smiles a wintry smile.*

*American* [*in a lull*]. How did it eventuate ?

*Little Man.* We got there just as the train was going to start ; and I jumped, thinking I could help her up. But it moved too quickly, and—and left her.

[*The gale of laughter blows up again.*

*American.* Guess I'd have thrown the baby out to her.

*Little Man.* I was afraid the poor little thing might break.

[*The* BABY *wails ; the* LITTLE MAN *heaves it ; the gale of laughter blows.*

*American* [*gravely*]. It's highly entertaining—not for the baby. What kind of an old baby is it, anyway ? [*He sniffs.*] I judge it's a bit—niffy.

*Little Man.* Afraid I've hardly looked at it yet.

*American.* Which end up is it ?

*Little Man.* Oh ! I think the right end. Yes, yes, it is.

*American.* Well, that's something. Maybe you should hold it out of window a bit. Very excitable things, babies !

*Englishwoman* [*galvanized*]. No, no !

*Englishman* [*touching her knee*]. My dear !

*American.* You are right, ma'am. I opine there's a draught out there. This baby is precious. We've all of us got stock in this baby in a manner of speaking. This is a little bit of universal brotherhood. Is it a woman baby ?

*Little Man.* I—I can only see the top of its head.

*American.* You can't always tell from that. It looks kind of over wrapped up. Maybe it had better be unbound.

*German.* Nein, nein, nein !

*American.* I think you are very likely right, colonel. It might be a pity to unbind that baby. I guess the lady should be consulted in this matter.

*Englishwoman.* Yes, yes, of course—I——

*Englishman* [*touching her*]. Let it be ! Little beggar seems all right.

*American.* That would seem only known to Providence at this moment. I judge it might be due to humanity to look at its face.

*Little Man* [*gladly*]. It's sucking my finger. There, there—nice little thing—there !

*American* [*addressing himself to the carriage at large.*] I think we may esteem ourselves fortunate to have this little stranger right here with us. Demonstrates what a hold the little and weak have upon us nowadays. The colonel here—a man of blood and iron—there he sits quite ca'm next door to it. [*He sniffs.*] Now, this baby is ruther chastening—that is a sign of grace, in the colonel—that is true heroism.

*Little Man* [*faintly*]. I—I can see its face a little now.                              [*All bend forward.*

*American.* What sort of a physiognomy has it, anyway ?

*Little Man* [*still faintly*]. I don't see anything but—but spots.

*German.* Oh ! Ha ! Pfui !

                              [*The* DUTCH YOUTH *laughs.*

*American.* I am told that is not uncommon amongst babies. Perhaps we could have you inform us, ma'am.

*Englishwoman.* Yes, of course—only—what sort of——

*Little Man.* They seem all over its—— [*At the slight recoil of every one*] I feel sure it's—it's quite a good baby underneath.

*American.* That will be ruther difficult to come at. I'm just a bit sensitive. I've very little use for affections of the epidermis.

*German.* Pfui ! [*He has edged away as far as he can get, and is lighting a big cigar.*]

[*The* DUTCH YOUTH *draws his legs back.*

*American* [*also taking a cigar*]. I guess it would be well to fumigate this carriage. Does it suffer, do you think ?

*Little Man* [*peering*]. Really, I don't—I'm not sure —I know so little about babies. I think it would have a nice expression—if—if it showed.

*American.* Is it kind of boiled-looking ?

*Little Man.* Yes—yes, it is.

*American* [*looking gravely round*]. I judge this baby has the measles.

[*The* GERMAN *screws himself spasmodically against the arm of the* ENGLISHWOMAN'S *seat.*

*Englishwoman.* Poor little thing ! Shall I——

[*She half rises.*

*Englishman* [*touching her*]. No, no—— Dash it !

*American.* I honour your emotion, ma'am. It does credit to us all. But I sympathize with your husband too. The measles is a very important pestilence in connection with a grown woman.

*Little Man.* It likes my finger awfully. Really, it's rather a sweet baby.

*American* [*sniffing*]. Well, that would appear to be quite a question. About them spots, now ? Are they rosy ?

*Little Man.* No-o ; they're dark, almost black.

*German.* Gott ! Typhus ! [*He bounds up on to the arm of the* ENGLISHWOMAN'S *seat.*]

*American.* Typhus ! That's quite an indisposition !

[*The* DUTCH YOUTH *rises suddenly, and bolts out into the corridor. He is followed by the* GERMAN, *puffing clouds of smoke. The* ENGLISH *and* AMERICAN *sit a moment longer without speaking. The* ENGLISHWOMAN'S *face is turned with a curious expression—half pity,*

*half fear—toward the* LITTLE MAN. *Then the*
ENGLISHMAN *gets up.*

*Englishman.* Bit stuffy for you here, dear, isn't it ?

[*He puts his arm through hers, raises her, and
almost pushes her through the doorway. She
goes, still looking back.*

*American* [*gravely.*] There's nothing I admire more'n
courage. Guess I'll go and smoke in the corridor.

[*As he goes out the* LITTLE MAN *looks very wistfully after him. Screwing up his mouth and
nose, he holds the* BABY *away from him and
wavers; then rising, he puts it on the seat
opposite and goes through the motions of letting
down the window. Having done so he looks at
the* BABY, *who has begun to wail. Suddenly he
raises his hands and clasps them, like a child
praying. Since, however, the* BABY *does not
stop wailing, he hovers over it in indecision;
then, picking it up, sits down again to dandle
it, with his face turned toward the open window.
Finding that it still wails, he begins to sing
to it in a cracked little voice. It is charmed
at once. While he is singing, the* AMERICAN
*appears in the corridor. Letting down the
passage window, he stands there in the doorway with the draught blowing his hair and the
smoke of his cigar all about him. The* LITTLE
MAN *stops singing; and shifts the shawl higher
to protect the* BABY'S *head from the draught.*

*American* [*gravely*]. This is the most sublime
spectacle I have ever envisaged. There ought to be
a record of this.

[*The* LITTLE MAN *looks at him, wondering.*
You are typical, sir, of the sentiments of modern
Christianity. You illustrate the deepest feelings in
the heart of every man.

[*The* LITTLE MAN *rises with the* BABY *and a movement of approach.*

Guess I'm wanted in the dining-car.    [*He vanishes.*
[*The* LITTLE MAN *sits down again, but back to the
    engine, away from the draught, and looks out
    of the window, patiently jogging the* BABY *on
    his knee.*

### CURTAIN

## SCENE III

*An arrival platform. The* LITTLE MAN, *with the*
BABY *and the bundle, is standing disconsolate, while
travellers pass and luggage is being carried by. A*
STATION OFFICIAL, *accompanied by a* POLICEMAN,
*appears from a doorway, behind him.*

*Official* [*consulting telegram in his hand*]. Das ist der
Herr.                [*They advance to the* LITTLE MAN.
*Official.* Sie haben einen Buben gestohlen ?
*Little Man.* I only speak English and American.
*Official.* Dies ist nicht Ihr Bube ?
                        [*He touches the* BABY.
*Little Man* [*shaking his head*]. Take care—it's ill.
                [*The man does not understand.*
Ill—the baby——
*Official* [*shaking his head*]. Verstehe nicht.  Dis is
nod your baby ?  No ?
*Little Man* [*shaking his head violently*]. No, it is
not.  No.
*Official* [*tapping the telegram*]. Gut ! You are
'rested.
    [*He signs to the* POLICEMAN, *who takes the* LITTLE
        MAN'S *arm.*
*Little Man.* Why ?  I don't want the poor baby.
*Official* [*lifting the bundle*]. Dies ist nicht Ihr Ge-
päck—pag ?
*Little Man.* No.

*Official.* Gut ! You are 'rested.

*Little Man.* I only took it for the poor woman. I'm not a thief—I'm—I'm——

*Official* [*shaking head*]. Verstehe nicht.

[*The* LITTLE MAN *tries to tear his hair. The disturbed* BABY *wails.*

*Little Man* [*dandling it as best he can*]. There, there —poor, poor !

*Official.* Halt still ! You are 'rested. It is all right.

*Little Man.* Where is the mother ?

*Official.* She komm by next drain. Das telegram say : Halt einen Herrn mit schwarzem Buben und schwarzem Gepäck. 'Rest gentleman mit black baby und black—pag.

[*The* LITTLE MAN *turns up his eyes to heaven.*

*Official.* Komm mit us.

[*They take the* LITTLE MAN *toward the door from which they have come. A voice stops them.*

*American* [*speaking from as far away as may be*]. Just a moment !

[*The* OFFICIAL *stops ; the* LITTLE MAN *also stops and sits down on a bench against the wall. The* POLICEMAN *stands stolidly beside him. The* AMERICAN *approaches a step or two, beckoning ; the* OFFICIAL *goes up to him.*

*American.* Guess you've got an angel from heaven there ! What's the gentleman in buttons for ?

*Official.* Was ist das ?

*American.* Is there anybody here that can understand American ?

*Official.* Verstehe nicht.

*American.* Well, just watch my gestures. I was saying [*he points to the* LITTLE MAN, *then makes gestures of flying*] you have an angel from heaven there. You have there a man in whom Gawd [*he points upward*] takes quite an amount of stock. You have no call to arrest him. [*He makes the gesture of arrest.*] No, sir. Providence has acted pretty mean, loading off that baby on him. [*He makes the motion of dand-ling.*] The little man has a heart of gold. [*He points to his heart, and takes out a gold coin.*]

*Official* [*thinking he is about to be bribed*]. Aber, das ist *zu* viel !

*American.* Now, don't rattle me ! [*Pointing to the* LITTLE MAN] Man [*pointing to his heart*] Herz [*pointing to the coin*] von Gold. This is a flower of the field—he don't want no gentleman in buttons to pluck him up.

[*A little crowd is gathering, including the* TWO ENGLISH, *the* GERMAN, *and the* DUTCH YOUTH.

*Official.* Verstehe absolut nichts. [*He taps the telegram.*] Ich muss mein duty do.

*American.* But I'm telling you. This is a white man. This is probably the whitest man on Gawd's earth.

*Official.* Das macht nichts—gut or no gut, I muss mein duty do. [*He turns to go towards the* LITTLE MAN.]

*American.* Oh ! Very well, arrest him ; do your duty. This baby has typhus.

[*At the word " typhus " the* OFFICIAL *stops.*

*American* [*making gestures*]. First-class typhus, black typhus, schwarzen typhus. Now you have it. I'm kind o' sorry for you and the gentleman in buttons. Do your duty !

*Official.* Typhus ? Der Bub'—die baby hat typhus ?

*American.* I'm telling you.

*Official.* Gott in Himmel !

*American* [*spotting the* GERMAN *in the little throng*]. Here's a gentleman will corroborate me.

*Official* [*much disturbed, and signing to the* POLICE-MAN *to stand clear*]. Typhus ! Aber das ist grässlich !

*American.* I kind o' thought you'd feel like that.

*Official.* Die Sanitätsmachine ! Gleich !

[*A* PORTER *goes to get it. From either side the broken half-moon of persons stand gazing at the* LITTLE MAN, *who sits unhappily dandling the* BABY *in the centre.*

*Official* [*raising his hands*]. Was zu thun ?

*American.* Guess you'd better isolate the baby.

> [*A silence, during which the* LITTLE MAN *is heard
> faintly whistling and clucking to the* BABY.

*Official* [*referring once more to his telegram*]. " 'Rest gentleman mit black baby." [*Shaking his head*] Wir must de gentleman hold. [*To the* GERMAN] Bitte, mein Herr, sagen Sie ihm, den Buben zu niedersetzen. [*He makes the gesture of deposit.*]

*German* [*to the* LITTLE MAN]. He say :  Put down the baby.

> [*The* LITTLE MAN *shakes his head, and continues to
> dandle the* BABY.

*Official.* You must.

> [*The* LITTLE MAN *glowers in silence.*

*Englishman* [*in background—muttering*]. Good man !

*German.* His spirit ever denies.

*Official* [*again making his gesture*]. Aber er muss !

> [*The* LITTLE MAN *makes a face at him.*

Sag' ihm :  Instantly put down baby, and komm mit us.                    [*The* BABY *wails.*

*Little Man.* Leave the poor ill baby here alone ? Be—be—be d——d to you !

*American* [*jumping on to a trunk—with enthusiasm*]. Bully !

> [*The* ENGLISH *clap their hands ; the* DUTCH YOUTH
> *laughs. The* OFFICIAL *is muttering, greatly
> incensed.*

*American.* What does that body-snatcher say ?

*German.* He say this man use the baby to save himself from arrest.  Very smart—he say.

*American.* I judge you do him an injustice. [*Showing off the* LITTLE MAN *with a sweep of his arm*] This is a white man.  He's got a black baby, and he won't leave it in the lurch.  Guess we would all act noble, that way, give us the chance.

> [*The* LITTLE MAN *rises, holding out the* BABY, *and
> advances a step or two.  The half-moon at once*

*gives, increasing its size ;  the* AMERICAN *climbs on to a higher trunk.  The* LITTLE MAN *retires and again sits down.*

*American* [*addressing the* OFFICIAL]. Guess you'd better go out of business and wait for the mother.

*Official* [*stamping his foot*]. Die Mutter sall 'rested be for taking out baby mit typhus.  Ha ! [*To the* LITTLE MAN] Put ze baby down !

[*The* LITTLE MAN *smiles.*
Do you 'ear ?

*American* [*addressing the* OFFICIAL]. Now, see here. 'Pears to me you don't suspicion just how beautiful this is.  Here we have a man giving his life for that old baby that's got no claim on him.  This is not a baby of his own.  No, sir, this is a very Christlike proposition in the gentleman.

*Official.* Put ze baby down, or ich will gommand some one it to do.

*American.* That will be very interesting to watch.

*Official* [*to* POLICEMAN]. Dake it vrom him.

[*The* POLICEMAN *mutters, but does not*

*American* [*to the* GERMAN]. Guess I lost that.

*German.* He say he is not his officier.

*American.* That just tickles me to death.

*Official* [*looking round*]. Vill nobody dake ze Bub' ?

*Englishwoman* [*moving a step—faintly*]. Yes—I——

*Englishman* [*grasping her arm*]. By Jove !  Will you !

*Official* [*gathering himself for a great effort to take the* BABY, *and advancing two steps*]. Zen I gommand you—— [*He stops and his voice dies away.*] Zit dere !

*American.* My !  That's wonderful.  What a man this is !  What a sublime sense of duty !

[*The* DUTCH YOUTH *laughs.  The* OFFICIAL *turns on him, but as he does so the* MOTHER *of the* BABY *is seen hurrying.*

*Mother.* Ach !  Ach !  Mei' Bubi !

[*Her face is illumined ; she is about to rush to the*
LITTLE MAN.

*Official* [*to the* POLICEMAN]. Nimm die Frau !

[*The* POLICEMAN *catches hold of the* WOMAN.

*Official* [*to the frightened* WOMAN]. Warum haben
Sie einen Buben mit Typhus mit ausgebracht ?

*American* [*eagerly, from his perch*]. What was that ?
I don't want to miss any.

*German.* He say : Why did you a baby with typhus
with you bring out ?

*American.* Well, that's quite a question.

[*He takes out the field-glasses slung around him and
adjusts them on the* BABY.

*Mother* [*bewildered*]. Mei' Bubi—Typhus—aber
Typhus ? [*She shakes her head violently.*] Nein, nein,
nein ! Typhus !

*Official.* Er hat Typhus.

*Mother* [*shaking her head*]. Nein, nein, nein !

*American* [*looking through his glasses*]. Guess she's
kind of right ! I judge the typhus is where the baby's
slobbered on the shawl, and it's come off on him.

[*The* DUTCH YOUTH *laughs.*

*Official* [*turning on him furiously*]. Er hat Typhus.

*American.* Now, that's where you slop over. Come
right here.

[*The* OFFICIAL *mounts, and looks through the glasses.*

*American* [*to the* LITTLE MAN]. Skin out the baby's
leg. If we don't locate spots on that, it'll be good
enough for me.

[*The* LITTLE MAN *fumbles out the* BABY'S *little
white foot.*

*Mother.* Mei' Bubi ! [*She tries to break away.*]

*American.* White as a banana. [*To the* OFFICIAL—
*affably*] Guess you've made kind of a fool of us with
your old typhus.

*Official.* Lass die Frau !

[*The* POLICEMAN *lets her go, and she rushes to her*
BABY.

*Mother.* Mei' Bubi !

> [*The* BABY, *exchanging the warmth of the* LITTLE
> MAN *for the momentary chill of its* MOTHER,
> *wails.*

*Official* [*descending and beckoning to the* POLICEMAN].
Sie wollen den Herrn accusiren ?

> [*The* POLICEMAN *takes the* LITTLE MAN'S *arm.*

*American.* What's that ? They goin' to pinch him
after all ?

> [*The* MOTHER, *still hugging her* BABY, *who has
> stopped crying, gazes at the* LITTLE MAN, *who
> sits dazedly looking up. Suddenly she drops
> on her knees, and with her free hand lifts his
> booted foot and kisses it.*

*American* [*waving his hat*]. Ra ! Ra ! [*He descends
swiftly, goes up to the* LITTLE MAN, *whose arm the*
POLICEMAN *has dropped, and takes his hand.*] Brother,
I am proud to know you. This is one of the greatest
moments I have ever experienced. [*Displaying the*
LITTLE MAN *to the assembled company*] I think I sense
the situation when I say that we all esteem it an
honour to breathe the rather inferior atmosphere of
this station here along with our little friend. I guess
we shall all go home and treasure the memory of his
face as the whitest thing in our museum of recollec-
tions. And perhaps this good woman will also go
home and wash the face of our little brother here. I
am inspired with a new faith in mankind. Ladies and
gentlemen, I wish to present to you a sure-enough
saint—only wants a halo, to be transfigured. [*To the*
LITTLE MAN] Stand right up.

> [*The* LITTLE MAN *stands up bewildered. They come
> about him. The* OFFICIAL *bows to him, the*
> POLICEMAN *salutes him. The* DUTCH YOUTH
> *shakes his head and laughs. The* GERMAN
> *draws himself up very straight, and bows
> quickly twice. The* ENGLISHMAN *and his* WIFE
> *approach at least two steps, then, thinking better*

*of it, turn to each other and recede. The* MOTHER
*kisses his hand. The* PORTER, *returning with
the* Sanitätsmachine, *turns it on from behind,
and its pinkish shower, goldened by a ray of
sunlight, falls around the* LITTLE MAN'S *head,
transfiguring it as he stands with eyes upraised
to see whence the portent comes.*

American [*rushing forward and dropping on his
knees*]. Hold on just a minute! Guess I'll take a
snapshot of the miracle. [*He adjusts his pocket
camera.*] This ought to look bully!

CURTAIN

# THE POETASTERS OF ISPAHAN

## By Clifford Bax

First produced on April 28th, 1912, at the Little Theatre by the Adelphi Play Society, under the management of Mr. MAURICE ELVEY, and with the following cast :

| | |
|---|---|
| HALLAJ, *the public letter-writer* | Mr. Maurice Elvey. |
| NEJRIHAL, *a pastry-cook* . . | Mr. Goodwin Nock. |
| ALA'D'DIN, *a perfume-seller* . | Mr. Bernard Merefield. |
| SULIMAN, *a barber* . . . | Mr. Ross Shore. |
| GULEESH, *a miserly silk-mercer* | Mr. Campbell Cargill. |
| IBN-HASSIM, *a wealthy jeweller* | Mr. James L. Dale. |
| SILVERMOON, *his daughter* . | Miss Betty Bellairs |
| SLAVE-BOY . . . . . | Mr. Gordon Gay. |
| FOUR NEGRO SLAVES | |

In the summer of 1912 the play was produced as a *lever de rideau* at the Criterion Theatre.

NOTE.—*There is no difficulty in dispensing with the Slave-boy and two of the Slaves, who have nothing to say.*

# THE POETASTERS OF ISPAHAN

[HALLAJ, *the public letter-writer, is discovered sitting in the centre of the room where he works. He is young and beautiful, but plainly gowned, for he is a poor man. Scrolls, reed-pens, and ribbons lie about him. On the floor are several rugs.*

*The room is represented by long dark curtains which divide at the back, both to right and left. These openings are supposed to look up to a street, and the light beyond them changes from amber to sapphire-blue, and again from blue to warm purple as the play proceeds. Two handsome copper lamps hang from the roof by long chains.*]

### HALLAJ [*to the audience*]

My friends—well met, and be of good cheer !
  For never, since Allah created man,
Was life more goodly to live than here
  In the city of Ispahan.
If I see one heart that retains a care,
  I will lower the curtain between us.  Why,
We are here so gay that we often say
  We cannot be sad though we try !
You meet me now in a sorry case,
But what is the use of a doleful face ?
Be sure I have done what I could to win
The maiden I love but have never seen !
  And why do I love her ?  Night and noon
I have lived with her sweet name—Silvermoon—
And surely a poet is hardly to blame
  If he falls in love with a name ?

143

My poem is done : but how to fulfil
The other part of her father's will ?
What did he say, with his merchant's wit ?
  " Ten pieces of silver must go with it,"—
And how to make one piece look like ten ?

> [*Holding up a single silver coin.*

Well—I share that trouble with wiser men !
So few come now to this shop of mine
That I scarcely hope for the other nine.
Well, well, it is folly to grumble.    See,
There is only this one coin left to me,
But that which is written by Fate—must be !

> [*A string of little bells is struck without, and a
> moment later* NEJRIHAL *enters through the
> curtain to the left.* HALLAJ *at once rises to
> greet him ceremoniously.*

### HALLAJ

Pray, pardon me, Nejrihal.    Had I but heard
  That you purposed a visit, my floor had been strewn
With jasmine and rose ; but you sent not a word.
  How is it you shut up your oven so soon ?

### NEJRIHAL

O Summit of Wisdom !    O Prince of the Pen !
  Is it true, as I have heard but a little while past
When I handed some dates to a party of men,
  That the rich Ibn-hassim has offered at last
His daughter for marriage ?

### HALLAJ

It is.

### NEJRIHAL

And they say
That he who shall make the most elegant verse
In praise of her beauty shall bear her away ?

HALLAJ

But the terms of the bargain could hardly be worse.

NEJRIHAL

What are they, Hallaj ?    For my part, I declare
  The whole city may go without supper to bed,
If a song shall obtain me a virgin as fair
  As the jeweller's daughter.    What is it he said ?

HALLAJ

You must finish your poem before the sun set.

NEJRIHAL

Well, well, that is good.    I have time and to spare,
For an hour, very nearly, remains to me yet.
Four lines and I've made it !    Why, once for the
      Sheikh
  I prepared a whole feast in the course of an hour,
And, bethink you, I fashioned and coloured each cake
In the form and the hue of some separate flower.
*That's* a feat to be proud of !    But tell me, I pray,
Is a verse the whole matter ?

HALLAJ

                              The name of the girl
Must be used as a rhyme for the rest, in the way
  That a jeweller imprisons an emerald or pearl
In foliage of silver or plumage of gold.

NEJRIHAL

  Or just as a pasty is made to the mould !
My poem . . . I feel it emerging . . .

HALLAJ

                              And then
You must write it in characters, clearly, like these.

NEJRIHAL

But you know that I never could manage a pen !

HALLAJ

Hallaj is your servant . . .

NEJRIHAL

But what are your fees ?

HALLAJ [*magniloquently*]

Why, sir, for a dinar of silver, I swear
   I will write it so finely that people shall cry
Of a beautiful maiden that passes them by,
   " She has looked on the poem of Nejrihal ! "

NEJRIHAL [*giving him a piece of silver*]

                There !
If it be as you say it is cheap at the price—
   But now for my poem.   Some clever device . . .
Let me think :  I will tell her that she is the lamp
   And I the poor moth—You upset me, my friend !
   What more does he want of me ?   Come, make an
      end !

HALLAJ

Ten pieces of silver !

NEJRIHAL

             The greedy old scamp !
No matter.   I'll pay them.   How I am the lamp
And she the poor moth as it flutters . . . no, no——
You have spoilt my whole poem.   Now, how did it
      go ?
   [*The bells are sounded again.   NEJRIHAL wanders
     off by himself, composing.*

HALLAJ

Who is there ?

VOICE WITHOUT

It is I, it is I, Ala'd'din,
The vendor of perfumes.

HALLAJ

Pray come in.

[ALA'D'DIN *enters through the curtain to the right,
unnoticed by* NEJRIHAL. *He is not handsome,
but being a great dandy, he makes his appearance conspicuous. His hair is arranged in
little ringlets. He is tall and angular, and has
small pointed features.*

HALLAJ

Truly this day
There must be junketing among my stars !
  For though the scent of roses may be sweet,
Ascending from your gay and gilded jars,
  Behold, I greet
One whose fine words are more to me than they.

ALA'D'DIN

If it be as you say,
Let us remember how the old proverb stands :
Work that is delicate makes for delicate hands.
But see . . . your friend !  He is not quite well, I
  fear ?

HALLAJ

Why, it is Nejrihal the confectioner.
Surely you must have seen him many a time ?

### ALA'D'DIN

I ?   Oh, dear no.   But tell me, why does he roll
So wildly ?

### HALLAJ

He is upon the Sea of Rhyme !

### ALA'D'DIN

What ?   What ?   A pastry-cook with a poet's soul ?
But can *he* really think to pipe the tune
That shall secure the sweet girl Silvermoon ?
Excellent !

### NEJRIHAL

What an infernal noise you make !
Oho, 'tis you, my old friend Ala'd'din !
You have never paid me for that sesame-cake !
   " Oh, crystal lamp that shows the flame within . . ."

### ALA'D'DIN

Trite, very trite.   Of him it might be said
His fancies are yet staler than his bread.
But come, Hallaj, and I'll make clear
The matter which has brought me here.
It seems that you have heard from him
Of the jeweller's eccentric whim ?

[HALLAJ *nods assent.*

Well, Ibn-hassim cannot read,
But—mark you !—like a vain old man
He is very proud indeed
Because his daughter can ;
Now Silvermoon——

### HALLAJ

I know, I know—
Will read the rhymes.

ALA'D'DIN

Exactly so.
What will you charge to write my verse ?

HALLAJ

Two silver pieces.

ALA'D'DIN

Two ?    Say one,
And, should I win, you take my purse ?

HALLAJ

That's a clean bargain.    Done !

NEJRIHAL [*beating his breast*]

Oh, I'm stuck fast !    I cannot reach that rhyme.

ALA'D'DIN [*gesticulating*]

Shall it be light ?  or passionate ?  or sublime ?

HALLAJ

Three pieces now.    The seven shall come in time !

ALA'D'DIN [*testily*]

Hallaj, I cannot possibly compose
With a creature near me pulling such a face
And fingering out his decimated prose.

HALLAJ [*very politely*]

Where would you like to sit ?

### ALA'D'DIN

In some soft place.
You have no cushions here.    Why, what a man . . .
You live like any Christian.

### HALLAJ

Sit you here.

### ALA'D'DIN

Eh ?  that were better !    Thank you . . . the divan.
And oh, Hallaj, if other folk appear,
Keep them away from me.    You cannot guess
How sensitive my brain is, how refined—
A vulgar phrase can give me keen distress,
A foolish face upsets me for a week.

[*Eyeing* NEJRIHAL.

### HALLAJ

Dear me, dear me !

### ALA'D'DIN

Now I'm beginning.    Mind !
[*The bells are sounded again to the right, with a
    frightful din.*

### HALLAJ

Another visitor—good.    Who is it ?    Speak !
[SULIMAN *comes rushing in, brandishing a large
    pair of scissors.  He is fat and has a round
    black beard.  Odds and ends pertaining to his
    profession are stuck here and there in his cos-
    tume.  He is much excited.*

### SULIMAN [*rapidly*]

Oh, Hallaj, have you heard ?  the old Jeweller ?  Well,
When the crier brought word to the street where I
    dwell,

I was off like a bird or a fiend out of Hell,
For the whole town is stirred by the story they tell !
She's a maiden for kings, a most marvellous prize—
Why, the worth of her rings you could hardly surmise,
For the gems that she brings are of such a great
    size . . .

HALLAJ [*good-humouredly*]

Don't brandish those things or you'll put out my eyes !

SULIMAN

But it's all like a trance !  I am so full of joy
That I feel I could dance as I did when a boy.
Come, grapple your chance—for I'll give you employ,
And I'll pay in advance though it be for a toy.
If I win her I swear, as I'm speaking to men,
That I'll never cut hair in my lifetime again !
Let me see, I'll prepare you my poem, and then
What I shall declare you shall write with your pen.

VOICE [*approaching rapidly down the street*]

You villain, come out !  Is it here that you hide ?
Hallaj, is the barber Suliman inside ?

SULIMAN [*in consternation*]

By Allah, Hallaj, when the crier appeared
I suppose I had only cut half of his beard !
    [*Enter* GULEESH, *a small insignificant man.  He is
    much agitated.  His beard is well trimmed on
    one side, but absurdly ragged on the other, and
    a coloured napkin is still tied round his neck.*

HALLAJ

Guleesh, you are welcome.

GULEESH

But why do you smile ?

HALLAJ

For a pleasure denied me a very long while.

GULEESH [*exploding*]

There he is !   By the grave of your fathers, you knave,
This trick is the maddest that ever I heard.
I am a man with a good reputation to save
    And you've made me look simply absurd.
Here I've sped through the street like a figure of fun
Nearly dead with the heat of the blistering sun,
And my beard incomplete !   It was only half done !
If you get near my feet I will teach you to run !

HALLAJ [*restraining him*]

No, no, my good fellow.   Come, listen to me.
He is not quite so bad as I think you suppose.
He is making a poem.

GULEESH

            A poem ?   What ! he ?
I will teach him to sing if I get at his nose !

ALA'D'DIN

You are really unbearable.   Clear him away

NEJRIHAL

There !   I've lost the one word that I counted upon.

SULIMAN [*soothingly*]

I will cut off the rest for you some other day—
Not now.   We are busy.   Begone !

HALLAJ

*[taking GULEESH by the shoulders and insisting that he
shall sit down in the last corner of the room]*

Be calm a moment, friend.    I have heard men say
You love a bargain.

GULEESH *[pricking up his ears]*

Well ?

HALLAJ

Then do as they.

GULEESH

What ?  make a poem ?   I ?

HALLAJ

Just four lines long.

You have heard the news ?

GULEESH

Of Ibn-hassim ?  yes.

He says he will sell his daughter for a song.
But girls are too expensive, I confess,
For my lean purse.

HALLAJ *[cunningly]*

Perhaps you have not heard. . . .

She has a hundred camels.

GULEESH

On your word ?

HALLAJ

A hundred at the least, and maybe more.

### GULEESH

What, and you did not tell me this before ?
Away !    I mean to win that girl.

### HALLAJ

No doubt,
But then your poem must be written out !

### GULEESH [*scratching his beard*]

Written ?  dear me.

### HALLAJ

One silver piece.    Now come !

### GULEESH

A silver piece ?   Too much.   Say half the sum.

### HALLAJ

But noble verses must be nobly penned.

### GULEESH [*flattered, but grudgingly*]

Well, here it is.

### HALLAJ

Think of her value, friend.

### ALA'D'DIN

At last a little quiet.   And now to get
Some new soul-dazzling rhyme for " Silvermoon."
Yes . . . let me think . . . I will thread the alphabet !
Boon ?  commonplace.  Coon, doon, buffoon, ghoon,
        hoon,
June—that might serve . . . loon, macaroon . . .
        noon, poon . . .

First fix your rhymes.   What though the sense be
    thin ?
Sound is the soul of song . . .

GULEESH [*from his corner*]

                    Tut, Ala'd'din,
Don't chatter so.   Just when I think I've caught
Some telling phrase, you dash it out of thought.

SULIMAN [*from his corner*]

Silence, Guleesh !   I am getting mine by heart.

NEJRIHAL [*from his corner*]

If you *must* talk I wish you would go apart.

ALA'D'DIN

How would that run ?   " The nightingale in June
Sings her desire . . ."

NEJRIHAL

                I think I have it now :
" The nightingale adores the Silver Moon . . ."

ALA'D'DIN [*rising*]

What's that you say ?   No, that I can't allow—
That was *my* thought—the nightingale !

GULEESH

                        So far
So good.   " What time the nightingale . . ."

ALA'D'DIN

                   You thieves !
You pack of pickbrains—that is what you are !

### HALLAJ

Why, what's amiss ?    Poets, and lovers too,
Quarrelling like the birds among the leaves ?
In this parched world you poets have always been
Like rain from heaven.    Come, this will never do !

### SULIMAN [*oblivious of the trouble*]

Hallaj, Guleesh, Nejrihal, Ala'd'din,
Listen !    I have made my quatrain.

### ALA'D'DIN

                          No, no, no,
This matter must be settled first. . . .

### SULIMAN

                          Away !
Put down my verses quickly before they go.
" Ah, thornless rose ! ah, cloudless plenilune !
Even as upon some soundless night in June
No nightingale . . ."

### ALA'D'DIN

                  What !  do you mean to say
*You've* got it too ?    Now, by my uncle's beard,
This is a rascally world !

### SULIMAN

                  What ?  " nightingale " ?
Of course I have got it—such a musical word !

### ALA'D'DIN

I had it first !

### NEJRIHAL

            You ?    It is mine !

### GULEESH

No—mine !

### HALLAJ

Now, all this bickering is of small avail—
Time presses. And, remember, if you will,
Though there be but one silver moon to shine,
In every garden when the warm night is still
She has her singing worshippers.

### SULIMAN

Well said !
There speaks a man of sense : and for my part,
I am willing, since the word is not my own,
To share it round with all of you instead.

### ALA'D'DIN

No, I refuse. I will not ! I protest !
Why, surely even to you it must be known
That repetition puts an end to art !

### SULIMAN

Well, you, Hallaj—having no interest,
No personal interest in this affair—
Decide between us what were for the best.

### NEJRIHAL

I'll hold to that.

### GULEESH

And I.

### ALA'D'DIN

And I—so there.

### HALLAJ

It is a simple matter. Let your verse
Be gay like noon or softly sad like dusk.

Or pompous like the star-attended dark—
Make it according to your desire, good sirs,
But . . . make it rich ; a paradise of words—
Perfumed with spikenard, cinnamon, myrrh, and
    musk,
And flowered like any royal garden-plot
With crimson lilies or lilies of the vale,
Hyacinth and rose.   Put in the names of birds,
Flamingoes, peacocks, parrots, the dove, the lark,
The popinjay—all that you will, but not,
No, not for love's sake, not the nightingale !

#### ALA'D'DIN

What, none of us ?   Well, it is hard on me . . .
But . . . as you will.

#### SULIMAN

                Then, do we all agree—
No nightingales ?   Good, now !   So let it be.
            [*They settle down again to composition.*

#### HALLAJ

One, two, three, four, five.
Heigho,
Behold the most unlucky man alive !
For I've heard it said by commercial men
That five is only the half of ten,
And I cannot imagine how to contrive
That *they* should give me the other five.
                        [*Addressing the audience.*
O Light of my Soul, I wonder what you,
If you were here would decide to do ?
There is none shall give her a better verse
(If I say what I in my heart believe),
But this want of coin is a cruel curse,
And I fear there is hardly time to thieve.
No matter !   If I can win her—well !

And if I lose I have yet the sun,
The clouds, and the earth whereon we dwell,
And flowers and poems and laughter . . .

### SULIMAN [*like the report of a cannon*]

                              Done !
Quickly, Hallaj !   Out with your pen and scroll !
The lines are like a torrent, mad to be gone,
And snarling at the cage-bars of my soul.
Quick !   Let us quench them !

### HALLAJ

                    Ready !   Steady !   On !

### SULIMAN

" Lo, with sharp wit my verses will I prune
With such nice art "—no, it had better be
" With such *keen* art, that, like a rose-festoon
Hung round her name . . ."

### NEJRIHAL [*hurrying up*]

                    Excellent !   Write for me
Swiftly these lines, Hallaj.   What was the rhyme ?
" As Jacob when he woke from sleep at noon . . ."

### SULIMAN

" Hung round her name, they shall let through their
        leaves . . ."

### HALLAJ

I cannot write with both hands.   Give me time.

### GULEESH [*running up*]

" Like rare silk spun within the poor cocoon . . .
These ten . . ."

ALA'D'DIN [*brushing them aside*]

Don't listen to a pack of thieves !
Come now.   Write out . . .

SULIMAN

I said, " Let through their leaves . . ."

ALA'D'DIN [*disregarding him*]

" As when some flute-girl pipes too suave a tune . . ."

GULEESH

" Like rare silk spun within the poor cocoon."

NEJRIHAL

" Held fast the Angel, crying, ' A boon ! a boon ! ' "

SULIMAN

" The sparkling radiance of my Silvermoon."

HALLAJ [*laughing*]

Stand off !   More room !   You are making me per-
        spire
With such a furnace of the heavenly fire.
One at a time, dear fellows, one at a time !
You were the first, Suliman ;  say me your rhyme.

SULIMAN

" Lo, by sharp wit my stanza will I prune
With such *deft* art, that, like a rose-festoon
Which hangs about her name, through every line
Shall burn the radiance of my Silvermoon."

HALLAJ

Charming and most adroit !   Would it were mine !

### ALA'D'DIN

Charming, you say ?    Adroit ?    Allah forbid !
*I* thought it clumsy . . .

### SULIMAN [*seizing him by an ear*]

Did you ?

### ALA'D'DIN

Let me go !

### HALLAJ

Now, Nejrihal, I am ready.    Lift up the lid.
What spicy cake of words have you to show ?

### NEJRIHAL

" As Jacob when he woke from sleep at noon
Held fast the Angel, crying ' A boon, a boon ! '
*I* will not lose the Angel of sweet rhyme,
Until he bless me with my Silvermoon."

### HALLAJ

Delightful—very.

### ALA'D'DIN

Nejrihal, my friend,
One word of counsel.    If you want to climb
Into her favour, see that you change the end.

### HALLAJ

Guleesh, come forward.    Count me out your verse.

### GULEESH

" Like rare silk spun within the poor cocoon,
The ten I pay shall spin a thousand soon !
Ten silver coins !    A hundred such were scarce
Too liberal pay for one such Silver Moon ! "
(2,797)

**11**

HALLAJ

Truly, with such a regal choice of wines,
Poor Silvermoon will scarce know which to drink !

ALA'D'DIN

There is too much talk of money in his lines.

HALLAJ

You are very hard to please.

ALA'D'DIN

You see, *I* think.
Neither by sound alone nor sense alone
Do I judge verse.

HALLAJ

Then let us hear your own.

ALA'D'DIN

Well . . . you insist.   But understand me, pray,
I count this a mere sketch, a rough design . . .
All genuine first-rate poets of our day
Take quite a week to squeeze out every line.
Thank you.   Ahem.   Well, these are the lines I made.
  " As when some flute-girl pipes too suave a tune,
  The soul, oppressed with joy, is like to swoon,
    So ere she speak I wait in happy dread
    To hear the golden voice of Silvermoon."

NEJRIHAL

A fancy like a mouse—your mind the cat !

SULIMAN

Fine as a razor's back !

GULEESH

So strong—like silk !

### HALLAJ

Quite as intoxicating as . . .

### ALA'D'DIN [*breathlessly*]

As what ?

### HALLAJ

Oh, as a bowl of . . . what shall I say ? . . . of milk !

### ALA'D'DIN

Milk ?  But I never heard it held before . . .

### SULIMAN [*gravely*]

Let us not mar the vague dusk of your verse
By lighting lamps of common speech.   No more.
Besides, there is not much time.   I must be gone
To fetch my coins.

### GULEESH

And I.   Quickly—disperse !

### NEJRIHAL

Farewell, Hallaj.   We shall be back anon.
              [*They all go out,* ALA'D'DIN *very perplexed.*

### HALLAJ

I will light the lamps . . . Ah, no.
   When the soft night falls on a day of heat
The pulse of a passionate heart beats low,
   And even sorrow is well-nigh sweet.
It were wiser to leave them so.

But away with your dreams, Hallaj !   Bestir,
And make your poor room ready for her.
How near each other are heaven and hell—
A handful of gold divides them !   Well,

I hope, whichever of these may win
It will not be that coxcomb Ala'd'din ;
Nor yet Guleesh, for they say the lives
Of camels are better than his poor wives' ;
And Nejrihal, though he bakes bread well,
Is a bit of a booby, truth to tell,
And I hate to picture, if he should win,
My Silvermoon with a rolling-pin !
No, no,
Since I myself can attain her not,
May she come to the good Suliman's lot.

> [*The curtain to the left is drawn a little aside. A
> face appears, then a body, then* NEJRIHAL *walks
> on tip-toe across the room.*

NEJRIHAL

Hallaj !

HALLAJ

        Who is it ?    To what do I owe
A second visit, my friend ?

NEJRIHAL

                        Speak low.
Is there any other beside you ?

HALLAJ
                        No.
I will light the lanterns to prove it . . . so.

NEJRIHAL

Let me tell you quickly.    I mean to win.
But I must confess that I do begin
To feel that my lines are a little thin
When set by the verses of Ala'd'din.
He is such a poet, you see, but I . . .
Well, briefly, a poem is not a pie.

You can give my hope an extended lease
With a stroke of your pen.   For a slight increase,
Will you turn his beautiful swans—to geese ?

HALLAJ (*taking up* ALA'D'DIN'S *poem*)

Let me see them.   Yes—for a silver piece !

NEJRIHAL

Why, then, I have won !  You shall have your pay . . .
And a junket, too, on the marriage-day !
　　　[*He steals out cautiously.   Just as he disappears a
　　　　face is seen peering round the curtain to the
　　　　right.   Then* SULIMAN *comes tip-toeing up to*
　　　　HALLAJ.

SULIMAN [*in a stage whisper*]

Hallaj !

HALLAJ [*turning*]

Who is it ?   Suliman ?

SULIMAN

　　　　　　　　　　　　Yes.

Hallaj, I am certain to fail unless
*You* will help in a scheme for my success.
Let me tell you . . .

HALLAJ

No matter.   I think I can guess.

SULIMAN

Well, before I explain, let me say at the start
That old Ibn-hassim cares little for art.
It is money he loves, and I fear for my part
That verse of Guleesh will go straight to his heart.
Now I pray you to lighten my pocket of this,
　　　　　　　　　　　　[*Giving him a coin.*

And then to abolish my difficulties
By leaving *my* verse for her just as it is,
And . . .

### HALLAJ

I quite understand.

### SULIMAN

Making rubbish of his !

[SULIMAN *chuckles as he creeps stealthily out of the
room.   A moment after he is gone the face of
GULEESH appears round the curtain to the right,
and simultaneously the face of* ALA'D'DIN *round
that to the left.*

### ALA'D'DIN

Hallaj !

### GULEESH

Hallaj !

### ALA'D'DIN

Who is there ?

### GULEESH

What, you ?

I come with a plea that is pressing.

### ALA'D'DIN

So ?

But mine, as it happens, is urgent too.

### GULEESH

Will you please to withdraw ?

### ALA'D'DIN

Will you kindly go ?

GULEESH

Alas, but that I can hardly do.

ALA'D'DIN

And with deep regret I must answer, No.

HALLAJ

Why then, come hither and hear me out,
   For a notable jest has occurred to me.
You both are resolved to win, no doubt ?
   But never could one man fight with three.
Now what were a silver coin from each
   If I, by twisting a phrase or word,
Should alter your rivals' elegant speech
   To the sorriest trash that you ever heard ?
I can do it—see—with a flourish here,
   With a line or the merest hyphen there,
And surely the price is not too dear
   For the gain of a girl so fair ?

ALA'D'DIN [*after a moment*]

By the beard of my cousin, you have more wit
Than I thought, Hallaj !   I agree to it.
                              [*He gives* HALLAJ *a coin.*

GULEESH [*a little dubiously*]

And I—though I fear there is just a touch
Of the fool within me to risk so much.
                              [*He gives* HALLAJ *a coin.*

ALA'D'DIN [*going out*]

Oh, Nehrijal, when I see your face
I shall laugh till the ribs of my body crack !
                              [*Exit left.*

GULEESH [*going out slowly*]

And though I may lose her, in either case,
You rogue, Suliman, I'll pay *you* back !

HALLAJ [*rapidly*]

One two, three, four,
Five, six, seven, eight,
Nine !
Just one piece more,
And oh, happy fate,
She is mine, mine, mine.
               [*Hurrying to the outlet on the right.*
Guleesh, turn back !   I must confess to you
That you have never driven a bargain worse.

GULEESH [*returning, furious*]

You rascal, then !   Pocketing my silver, too.

HALLAJ

He who makes perfume readily makes verse.
Ala'd'din is a poet.   I am afraid
Your quatrain hits the target somewhat low.

GULEESH

Give me back, then, the monies that I have paid !

HALLAJ

Guleesh, Guleesh, are you so dull ?   No, no,—
Do they not say it is the final sprint
That wins a race ?   Of course, do what you please . . .
But . . . for one more coin from the Sultan's mint . . .

GULEESH

You will serve Ala'd'din as you served these ?
You swear it ?

HALLAJ

Yes, I swear it . . . by your beard !
See, 'tis already done.

GULEESH

What, with one word ?

HALLAJ

Wait, wait, Guleesh, till Silvermoon shall come.
Then you shall see.

GULEESH

It is so large a sum

HALLAJ [*indifferently*]

Well, as you will.   I know you are money-wise,
But think, my friend, what wealth comes with the
        prize !
You waver ?   You refuse ?   Then be it so.
I hear a noise of bells.   You have lost her !

GULEESH [*with an effort, giving another coin*]

No !

HALLAJ

Ten !   Ten at last !

GULEESH

I do not understand . . .

Ten what ?

HALLAJ

Why . . . blessings on your princely hand.
        [*Going to the curtain right, and looking out.*
See how the blue unhappy dusk departs !
I feel the moonrise.   Oh, if the world of men

Might but remain for ever half so sweet,
And we with youth and love kindling our hearts,
Life were a poem, so beautiful, so complete,
That every poet might put down his pen !

### GULEESH

You speak as though *you* thought to win her

### HALLAJ

Yes,
I am very much the dreamer, I confess,
But life is what we make it, and in truth
'Tis not worth having when we forget our youth
But listen !   Do you not hear a noise of feet,
And of the bells upon her palanquin
Coming toward us down the little street

> [*The suitors enter.*

And here her poet-lovers.   Welcome in.

### NEJRIHAL [*excitedly*]

Near by the mosque, Hallaj, we saw her pass !

### SULIMAN

She is lovelier than an almond-tree in bloom !

### ALA'D'DIN

Prithee, Hallaj, have you no looking-glass ?

### HALLAJ

No, none.   Bestir yourselves now.   Give her room !

> [*Two black slaves enter, pull back the curtains on the right, and stand on either side of it.*
> IBN-HASSIM *enters slowly.   He is old and dignified, with a face so fine that it gives the lie at once to* SULIMAN'S *fear that " it is money he*

*loves." He is followed by a palanquin, richly
hung with green and crimson silks, and borne by
two tall slaves. They set it down just outside
the entrance. SILVERMOON rises out of her
cushions, tall, dark, and full-formed. She is
dressed in black and silver, and bears a diamond
moon on her brow. Two more slaves bring up
the rear, carrying wooden caskets of indescribable
beauty. IBN-HASSIM takes SILVERMOON by the
hand and leads her to the divan, where they sit
down. The slaves stand in a row behind them.*

### IBN-HASSIM

Citizens of our blue-domed Ispahan,
I need not much detain you.   What I have said
You have all heard.   I am an old, grey man,
Now grown desirous that my child should wed
Before my years are over.   Should you ask
Wherefore I sell my daughter for a song,
In place of setting you some soldier's task
To prove your worth, my answer is not long.
If a man love not poetry, the bloom
And fragrance of all life, nor have no shame,
I count him so unnatural from the womb,
So brutish, that he is but man in name !
Thus, too, I know that he whose heart has bowed
To beauty, howsoever else he errs,
Will prove more tender than the swinish crowd,
More musically-minded.   Therefore, sirs,
Each in due turn advance.   Let us behold
Which of you stands most excellent in verse.
He shall be dowered with beauty and with gold.

### HALLAJ [*to* SILVERMOON, *giving her the scrolls*]

Though they be written by an unworthy pen,
O Moon of April, deign to look on these.

SILVERMOON (*loving at first sight*)
You are Hallaj, the Prince of Writers, then ?

HALLAJ
Prince ?    Yes, if now my penmanship shall please.

SILVERMOON
The scroll I take bears at its foot the name
Of Nejrihal.

NEJRIHAL
If it please you, I am the same.
The verses are a trifle thin, I fear,
But " first-rate " poets . . .

IBN-HASSIM
Silence !    We wait to hear.

SILVERMOON [*reading*]
" If you but wed with me, bright Silvermoon . . ."

NEJRIHAL
What ?  but I never made . . .

IBN-HASSIM
Be silent, sir !

SILVERMOON
" If you but wed with me, bright Silvermoon,
Think how the whole year through from June to June,
    You shall eat raisins, candy, and sugar-cakes,
And lick the honey from my cooking-spoon ! "
                    [*Turning to* IBN-HASSIM, *with a smile.*
My lord, 'tis clear, however well he bakes,
Here is no poet !

NEJRIHAL

But . . . but . . . but I swear
I never made a word of what is there.
Hallaj, you are a scoundrel !   Allah forbid
That I should make a verse like that !

ALA'D'DIN *and* GULEESH

You did !

NEJRIHAL

Sir, I protest.   Their joke has gone too far.
These verses are not mine !

ALA'D'DIN *and* GULEESH

Oh, yes, they are !

NEJRIHAL

Am I enchanted ?   What ?   I am most perplexed.
I am sure I never made them.

IBN-HASSIM

Come !   The next !

SILVERMOON

Suliman is the name that we descry
Upon this manuscript.   Which is he ?

SULIMAN

I !

SILVERMOON (*reading*)

" If thou accept . . ."

SULIMAN

No, no . . . " Lo, by sharp wit . . ."

#### IBN-HASSIM

Not a word more !   Daughter, proceed with it.

#### SILVERMOON [*reading*]

" If thou accept my verse, O Silvermoon,
I'll hang about thee like a rose-festoon.
  Behold, my heart is like a lamp new-lit,
My corporal shape,—well, like a kind baboon ! "

#### SULIMAN [*breaking from the others*]

Where is Hallaj ?   I'll cut your throat next time
I get at you, for penning such a rhyme !
I'll whip you into lather !

#### HALLAJ [*whispering*]

                    Just a word.

#### SULIMAN

What ?  well—why, that's the merriest quip I've
      heard !

#### IBN-HASSIM

'Tis very plain these babblers cannot win.
Read me the others.   Come now.

#### SILVERMOON

                              Ala'd'din.

#### ALA'D'DIN

Permit me to suggest that you should read
My poor lame verses with a careful heed
To their entire effect.   To make the part
Outshine the whole,—that is a *crime* in art.

#### GULEESH

Rare, rare, oh rare !   He'll find he spoke too soon !

SILVERMOON [*reading*]

" I am no haggling dwarf, O Silvermoon . . ."

ALA'D'DIN

" No haggling dwarf . . . ? "

IBN-HASSIM [*furiously, to a slave boy*]

Go you and hold his tongue !

SILVERMOON (*reading*)

" No pastry-cook, no boisterous, black buffoon.
  I am so finely-tempered, so high-strung,
That, having made this verse for you, I swoon ! "
                                    [*To* IBN-HASSIM.
Bid me not marry with such a thing as this—
This toyman !   One might *kill* him with a kiss !
There is but one more scroll.   " Guleesh."

IBN-HASSIM

                                    To you,
Good sir, it seems the poet's prize is due,
For since it could not possibly be worse
Than these, there is no cause to read your verse.
Take her . . .

SILVERMOON

But, father, look . . . he squints !

GULEESH

                                    I pray
That you will not so lightly fling away
One whole hour's labour.   No, it were hard indeed.
I take it ill.

SILVERMOON [*glancing down the scroll*]

            Most gladly will I read.        [*Reading*.
" Like rare silk spun within the poor cocoon,

The ten I pay shall spin a thousand soon—
And yet—maybe the stuff's not worth the price !
What ! shall I pay all this for Silvermoon ? "

GULEESH

Give up my coins, Hallaj !    Three pieces !

SULIMAN [*dragging him down*]

Friend,
If you would win them back, take my advice,
And sit you down.    We have not heard the end
Of this good story.

HALLAJ

Oh, we have made her cry.

SILVERMOON [*through her tears*]

They have all mocked at me.

HALLAJ

" They ? " it was I !

IBN-HASSIM

You, sir ?    Explain—or else I'll have your head !

HALLAJ

Behold, another poem as yet unread.

IBN-HASSIM

Who made it ?

HALLAJ

I.

IBN-HASSIM

They told me you were poor.
Have you ten silver pieces, then ?

HALLAJ

For sure !
Take them and all I have,—my writing skill,
My strength, my youth, my laughter, what you will,
And what I can,—my wit in word or deed,
And, best, my poet's joy of beauty !

IBN-HASSIM

Read !

SILVERMOON

I will not even hear his rhyme, unless——

SULIMAN

Unless Hallaj himself shall read it ?

SILVERMOON

Yes.

SULIMAN [*to* IBN-HASSIM]

Sir, may the writer read ?

IBN-HASSIM

Let it be so.

HALLAJ [*reciting*]

" Tender and sweet like placid water strewn
With fluttering moonflakes on a night of June,
   Are all her thoughts and all her words, for lo !
There in mid-heaven the soul of Silvermoon ! "

SILVERMOON

Oh, it is beautiful !

SULIMAN

A most charming verse
Dear fellow, so original, so terse—
Is it not, Ala'd'din ?

12

ALA'D'DIN

It is very good.

IBN-HASSIM

Why, then, my plan has ended as it should,
In general harmony.   Now, Hallaj, my son,
Receive the gentle prize that you have won,
First by your wit and after by your song !
May you both live melodiously and long,
Hallaj and Silvermoon, poet and wife,
Linked in such love that, when our share of life
Has faded into the dreamy past of man,
Folk shall remember the Lovers of Ispahan.
    As for this trumpery, why, it is of earth ;
I did but ask for it to prove your worth,
In sign whereof (give me the cask) behold !
How I transmute your silver into gold.

HALLAJ

But one word more.    Forgive the trick I played
On you, my friends.    Let recompense be made.
Guleesh, I give you these (yes, the whole purse !)
For you shall still make money by your verse.
You, Ala'd'din, shall have a satin gown
The twin of which has no man in the town.
And as for Nejrihal, what shall I say ?  . . .
Ah yes, " a junket on the marriage day."
What for Suliman ?  something fair and fine . . .

SULIMAN

Give me your love.

HALLAJ

I give it.

SILVERMOON

And I mine.

# RIDERS TO THE SEA

## By J. M. Synge

# CHARACTERS

MAURYA, *an old woman.*
BARTLEY, *her son.*
CATHLEEN, *her daughter.*
NORA, *a younger daughter.*
MEN AND WOMEN.

SCENE.—*An island off the West of Ireland.*

This play was first performed in the Molesworth Hall, Dublin, on February 25, 1904, with the following cast :

MAURYA . . . . . . . Honor Lavelle.
BARTLEY . . . . . . . W. G. Fay.
CATHLEEN . . . . . . Sara Allgood.
NORA . . . . . . . Emma Vernon.

# RIDERS TO THE SEA

[*Cottage kitchen, with nets, oilskins, spinning-wheel, some new boards standing by the wall, etc.* CATHLEEN, *a girl of about twenty, finishes kneading cake, and puts it down in the pot-oven by the fire ; then wipes her hands, and begins to spin at the wheel.* NORA, *a young girl, puts her head in at the door.*]

*Nora* [*in a low voice*]. Where is she ?

*Cathleen.* She's lying down, God help her, and maybe sleeping, if she's able.

[NORA *comes in softly and takes a bundle from under her shawl.*

*Cathleen* [*spinning the wheel rapidly*]. What is it you have ?

*Nora.* The young priest is after bringing them. It's a shirt and a plain stocking were got off a drowned man in Donegal.

[CATHLEEN *stops her wheel with a sudden movement, and leans out to listen.*

We're to find out if it's Michael's they are, some time herself will be down looking by the sea.

*Cathleen.* How would they be Michael's, Nora ? How would he go the length of that way to the far north ?

*Nora.* The young priest says he's known the like of it. " If it's Michael's they are," says he, " you can tell herself he's got a clean burial, by the grace of God ; and if they're not his, let no one say a word about them, for she'll be getting her death," says he, " with crying and lamenting."

[*The door which* Nora *half closed is blown open by a gust of wind.*

*Cathleen* [*looking out anxiously*]. Did you ask him would he stop Bartley going this day with the horses to the Galway fair ?

*Nora.* " I won't stop him," says he ; " but let you not be afraid. Herself does be saying prayers half through the night, and the Almighty God won't leave her destitute," says he, " with no son living."

*Cathleen.* Is the sea bad by the white rocks, Nora ?

*Nora.* Middling bad, God help us. There's a great roaring in the west, and it's worse it'll be getting when the tide's turned to the wind. [*She goes over to the table with the bundle.*] Shall I open it now ?

*Cathleen.* Maybe she'd wake up on us, and come in before we'd done [*coming to the table*]. It's a long time we'll be, and the two of us crying.

*Nora* [*goes to the inner door and listens*]. She's moving about on the bed. She'll be coming in a minute.

*Cathleen.* Give me the ladder, and I'll put them up in the turf-loft, the way she won't know of them at all, and maybe when the tide turns she'll be going down to see would he be floating from the east.

[*They put the ladder against the gable of the chimney ;* Cathleen *goes up a few steps and hides the bundle in the turf-loft.* Maurya *comes from the inner room.*

*Maurya* [*looking up at* Cathleen *and speaking querulously*]. Isn't it turf enough you have for this day and evening ?

*Cathleen.* There's a cake baking at the fire for a short space [*throwing down the turf*], and Bartley will want it when the tide turns if he goes to Connemara.

[Nora *picks up the turf and puts it round the pot-oven.*

*Maurya* [*sitting down on a stool at the fire*]. He won't

go this day with the wind rising from the south and west. He won't go this day, for the young priest will stop him surely.

*Nora.* He'll not stop him, mother; and I heard Eamon Simon and Stephen Pheety and Colum Shawn saying he would go.

*Maurya.* Where is he itself?

*Nora.* He went down to see would there be another boat sailing in the week, and I'm thinking it won't be long till he's here now, for the tide's turning at the green head, and the hooker's tacking from the east.

*Cathleen.* I hear some one passing the big stones.

*Nora* [*looking out*]. He's coming now, and he in a hurry.

*Bartley* [*comes in and looks round the room; speaking sadly and quietly*]. Where is the bit of new rope, Cathleen, was bought in Connemara?

*Cathleen* [*coming down*]. Give it to him, Nora; it's on a nail by the white boards. I hung it up this morning, for the pig with the black feet was eating it.

*Nora* [*giving him a rope*]. Is that it, Bartley?

*Maurya.* You'd do right to leave that rope, Bartley, hanging by the boards. [BARTLEY *takes the rope.*] It will be wanting in this place, I'm telling you, if Michael is washed up to-morrow morning, or the next morning, or any morning in the week; for it's a deep grave we'll make him, by the grace of God.

*Bartley* [*beginning to work with the rope*]. I've no halter the way I can ride down on the mare, and I must go now quickly. This is the one boat going for two weeks or beyond it, and the fair will be a good fair for horses, I heard them saying below.

*Maurya.* It's a hard thing they'll be saying below if the body is washed up and there's no man in it to make the coffin, and I after giving a big price for the finest white boards you'd find in Connemara.

[*She looks round at the boards.*

*Bartley.* How would it be washed up, and we after

looking each day for nine days, and a strong wind blowing a while back from the west and south ?

*Maurya.* If it isn't found itself, that wind is raising the sea, and there was a star up against the moon, and it rising in the night. If it was a hundred horses, or a thousand horses, you had itself, what is the price of a thousand horses against a son where there is one son only.

*Bartley* [*working at the halter, to* CATHLEEN]. Let you go down each day, and see the sheep aren't jumping in on the rye, and if the jobber comes you can sell the pig with the black feet if there is a good price going.

*Maurya.* How would the like of her get a good price for a pig ?

*Bartley* [*to* CATHLEEN]. If the west wind holds with the last bit of the moon let you and Nora get up weed enough for another cock for the kelp. It's hard set we'll be from this day with no one in it but one man to work.

*Maurya.* It's hard set we'll be surely the day you're drowned with the rest. What way will I live and the girls with me, and I an old woman looking for the grave ?

[BARTLEY *lays down the halter, takes off his old coat, and puts on a newer one of the same flannel.*

*Bartley* [*to* NORA]. Is she coming to the pier ?

*Nora* [*looking out*]. She's passing the green head and letting fall her sails.

*Bartley* [*getting his purse and tobacco*]. I'll have half an hour to go down, and you'll see me coming again in two days, or in three days, or maybe in four days if the wind is bad.

*Maurya* [*turning round to the fire and putting the shawl over her head*]. Isn't it a hard and cruel man won't hear a word from an old woman, and she holding him from the sea ?

*Cathleen.* It's the life of a young man to be going on the sea, and who would listen to an old woman with one thing and she saying it over?

*Bartley* [*taking the halter*]. I must go now quickly. I'll ride down on the red mare, and the grey pony 'll run behind me. . . . The blessing of God on you.

[*He goes out.*

*Maurya* [*crying out as he is in the door*]. He's gone now, God spare us, and we'll not see him again. He's gone now, and when the black night is falling I'll have no son left me in the world.

*Cathleen.* Why wouldn't you give him your blessing and he looking round in the door? Isn't it sorrow enough is on every one in this house without your sending him out with an unlucky word behind him, and a hard word in his ear?

[MAURYA *takes up the tongs and begins raking the fire aimlessly without looking round.*

*Nora* [*turning towards her*]. You're taking away the turf from the cake.

*Cathleen* [*crying out*]. The Son of God forgive us, Nora, we're after forgetting his bit of bread.

[*She comes over to the fire.*

*Nora.* And it's destroyed he'll be going till dark night, and he after eating nothing since the sun went up.

*Cathleen* [*turning the cake out of the oven*]. It's destroyed he'll be, surely. There's no sense left on any person in a house where an old woman will be talking for ever. [MAURYA *sways herself on her stool.*

*Cathleen* [*cutting off some of the bread and rolling it in a cloth; to* MAURYA]. Let you go down now to the spring well and give him this and he passing. You'll see him then and the dark word will be broken, and you can say " God speed you," the way he'll be easy in his mind.

*Maurya* [*taking the bread*]. Will I be in it as soon as himself?

*Cathleen.* If you go now quickly.

*Maurya* [*standing up unsteadily*]. It's hard set I am to walk.

*Cathleen* [*looking at her anxiously*]. Give her the stick, Nora, or maybe she'll slip on the big stones.

*Nora.* What stick?

*Cathleen.* The stick Michael brought from Connemara.

*Maurya* [*taking a stick* NORA *gives her*]. In the big world the old people do be leaving things after them for their sons and children, but in this place it is the young men do be leaving things behind for them that do be old.

[*She goes out slowly.* NORA *goes over to the ladder*.

*Cathleen.* Wait, Nora, maybe she'd turn back quickly. She's that sorry, God help her, you wouldn't know the thing she'd do.

*Nora.* Is she gone round by the bush?

*Cathleen* [*looking out*]. She's gone now. Throw it down quickly, for the Lord knows when she'll be out of it again.

*Nora* [*getting the bundle from the loft*]. The young priest said he'd be passing to-morrow, and we might go down and speak to him below if it's Michael's they are surely.

*Cathleen* [*taking the bundle*]. Did he say what way they were found?

*Nora* [*coming down*]. " There were two men," says he, " and they rowing round with poteen before the cocks crowed, and the oar of one of them caught the body, and they passing the black cliffs of the north."

*Cathleen* [*trying to open the bundle*]. Give me a knife, Nora; the string's perished with the salt water, and there's a black knot on it you wouldn't loosen in a week.

*Nora* [*giving her a knife*]. I've heard tell it was a long way to Donegal.

*Cathleen* [*cutting the string*]. It is surely. There was

a man in here a while ago—the man sold us that knife—
and he said if you set off walking from the rocks beyond, it would be in seven days you'd be in Donegal.

*Nora.* And what time would a man take, and he
floating?

[CATHLEEN *opens the bundle and takes out a bit of
a shirt and a stocking. They look at them
eagerly.*

*Cathleen* [*in a low voice*]. The Lord spare us, Nora!
isn't it a queer hard thing to say if it's his they are
surely?

*Nora.* I'll get his shirt off the hook the way we can
put the one flannel on the other. [*She looks through
some clothes hanging in the corner.*] It's not with them,
Cathleen, and where will it be?

*Cathleen.* I'm thinking Bartley put it on him in the
morning, for his own shirt was heavy with the salt in
it. [*Pointing to the corner*] There's a bit of a sleeve was
of the same stuff. Give me that and it will do. [NORA
*brings it to her and they compare the flannel.*] It's the same
stuff, Nora; but if it is itself aren't there great rolls
of it in the shops of Galway, and isn't it many another
man may have a shirt of it as well as Michael himself?

NORA [*who has taken up the stocking and counted
the stitches, crying out*]. It's Michael, Cathleen, it's
Michael; God spare his soul, and what will herself say
when she hears this story, and Bartley on the sea?

*Cathleen* [*taking the stocking*]. It's a plain stocking.

*Nora.* It's the second one of the third pair I knitted,
and I put up three-score stitches, and I dropped four
of them.

*Cathleen* [*counts the stitches*]. It's that number is in
it [*crying out*]. Ah, Nora, isn't it a bitter thing to think
of him floating that way to the far north, and no one
to keen * him but the black hags that do be flying on
the sea?

*Nora* [*swinging herself half round, and throwing out*

* *Keen*, lament and wail for the dead.

*her arms on the clothes*]. And isn't it a pitiful thing when there is nothing left of a man who was a great rower and fisher but a bit of an old shirt and a plain stocking?

*Cathleen* [*after an instant*]. Tell me is herself coming, Nora? I hear a little sound on the path.

*Nora* [*looking out*]. She is, Cathleen. She's coming up to the door.

*Cathleen.* Put these things away before she'll come in. Maybe it's easier she'll be after giving her blessing to Bartley, and we won't let on we've heard anything the time he's on the sea.

*Nora* [*helping* CATHLEEN *to close the bundle*]. We'll put them here in the corner.

[*They put them into a hole in the chimney-corner.*
CATHLEEN *goes back to the spinning-wheel.*

*Nora.* Will she see it was crying I was?

*Cathleen.* Keep your back to the door the way the light 'll not be on you.

[NORA *sits down at the chimney-corner, with her back to the door.* MAURYA *comes in very slowly, without looking at the girls, and goes over to her stool at the other side of the fire. The cloth with the bread is still in her hand. The girls look at each other, and* NORA *points to the bundle of bread.*

*Cathleen* [*after spinning for a moment*]. You didn't give him his bit of bread?

[MAURYA *begins to keen softly, without turning round.*

*Cathleen.* Did you see him riding down?

[MAURYA *goes on keening.*

*Cathleen* [*a little impatiently*]. God forgive you; isn't it a better thing to raise your voice and tell what you seen, than to be making lamentation for a thing that's done? Did you see Bartley, I'm saying to you?

*Maurya* [*with a weak voice*]. My heart's broken from this day.

*Cathleen* [*as before*]. Did you see Bartley?

*Maurya*. I seen the fearfullest thing.

*Cathleen* [*leaves her wheel and looks out*]. God forgive you ; he's riding the mare now over the green head, and the grey pony behind him.

*Maurya* [*starts, so that her shawl falls back from her head and shows her white tossed hair. With a frightened voice*]. The grey pony behind him . . .

*Cathleen* [*coming to the fire*]. What is it ails you at all ?

*Maurya* [*speaking very slowly*]. I've seen the fearfullest thing any person has seen since the day Bride Dara seen the dead man with the child in his arms.

*Cathleen and Nora*. Uah.

> [*They crouch down in front of the old woman at the fire.*

*Nora*. Tell us what it is you seen.

*Maurya*. I went down to the spring well, and I stood there saying a prayer to myself. Then Bartley came along, and he riding on the red mare with the grey pony behind him [*she puts up her hands as if to hide something from her eyes*]. The Son of God spare us, Nora !

*Cathleen*. What is it you seen ?

*Maurya*. I seen Michael himself.

*Cathleen* [*speaking softly*]. You did not, mother. It wasn't Michael you seen, for his body is after being found in the far north, and he's got a clean burial, by the grace of God.

*Maurya* [*a little defiantly*]. I'm after seeing him this day, and he riding and galloping. Bartley came first on the red mare, and I tried to say " God speed you," but something choked the words in my throat. He went by quickly ; and " The blessing of God on you," says he, and I could say nothing. I looked up then, and I crying, at the grey pony, and there was Michael upon it—with fine clothes on him, and new shoes on his feet.

*Cathleen* [*begins to keen*]. It's destroyed we are from this day. It's destroyed, surely.

*Nora.* Didn't the young priest say the Almighty God won't leave her destitute with no son living?

*Maurya* [*in a low voice, but clearly*]. It's little the like of him knows of the sea. . . . Bartley will be lost now, and let you call in Eamon and make me a good coffin out of the white boards, for I won't live after them. I've had a husband, and a husband's father, and six sons in this house—six fine men, though it was a hard birth I had with every one of them and they coming to the world—and some of them were found and some of them were not found, but they're gone now the lot of them. . . . There were Stephen and Shawn were lost in the great wind, and found after in the Bay of Gregory of the Golden Mouth, and carried up the two of them on one plank, and in by that door.

[*She pauses for a moment, the girls start as if they heard something through the door that is half open behind them.*

*Nora* [*in a whisper*]. Did you hear that, Cathleen? Did you hear a noise in the north-east?

*Cathleen* [*in a whisper*]. There's some one after crying out by the seashore.

*Maurya* [*continues without hearing anything*]. There was Sheamus and his father, and his own father again, were lost in a dark night, and not a stick or sign was seen of them when the sun went up. There was Patch after was drowned out of a curragh that was turned over. I was sitting here with Bartley, and he a baby lying on my two knees, and I seen two women, and three women, and four women coming in, and they crossing themselves and not saying a word. I looked out then, and there were men coming after them, and they holding a thing in the half of a red sail, and water dripping out of it—it was a dry day, Nora—and leaving a track to the door.

[*She pauses again with her hand stretched out to-*

*wards the door. It opens softly and old women*
*begin to come in, crossing themselves on the*
*threshold, and kneeling down in front of the*
*stage with red petticoats over their heads.*

*Maurya [half in a dream, to* CATHLEEN*].* Is it Patch,
or Michael, or what is it at all?

*Cathleen.* Michael is after being found in the far
north, and when he is found there how could he be
here in this place?

*Maurya.* There does be a power of young men floating round in the sea, and what way would they know if
it was Michael they had, or another man like him, for
when a man is nine days in the sea, and the wind
blowing, it's hard set his own mother would be to say
what man was in it.

*Cathleen.* It's Michael, God spare him, for they're
after sending us a bit of his clothes from the far north.

*[She reaches out and hands* MAURYA *the clothes that*
*belonged to* MICHAEL. MAURYA *stands up*
*slowly and takes them in her hands.* NORA
*looks out.*

*Nora.* They're carrying a thing among them, and
there's water dripping out of it and leaving a track
by the big stones.

*Cathleen [in a whisper to the women who have come*
*in].* Is it Bartley it is?

*One of the Women.* It is surely, God rest his soul.

*[Two younger women come in and pull out the table.*
*Then men carry in the body of* BARTLEY, *laid on*
*a plank, with a bit of sail over it, and lay it on*
*the table.*

*Cathleen [to the women as they are doing so].* What
way was he drowned?

*One of the Women.* The grey pony knocked him over
into the sea, and he was washed out where there is a
great surf on the white rocks.

*[*MAURYA *has gone over and knelt down at the*
*head of the table. The women are keening softly*

*and swaying themselves with a slow movement.*
CATHLEEN *and* NORA *kneel at the other end of the table. The men kneel near the door.*

MAURYA [*raising her head and speaking as if she did not see the people around her*]. They're all gone now, and there isn't anything more the sea can do to me. . . . I'll have no call now to be up crying and praying when the wind breaks from the south, and you can hear the surf is in the east, and the surf is in the west, making a great stir with the two noises, and they hitting one on the other. I'll have no call now to be going down and getting Holy Water in the dark nights after Samhain, and I won't care what way the sea is when the other women will be keening. [*To* NORA] Give me the Holy Water, Nora; there's a small sup still on the dresser.

[NORA *gives it to her.*

MAURYA [*drops* MICHAEL'S *clothes across* BARTLEY'S *feet, and sprinkles the Holy Water over him*]. It isn't that I haven't prayed for you, Bartley, to the Almighty God. It isn't that I haven't said prayers in the dark night till you wouldn't know what I'd be saying; but it's a great rest I'll have now, and it's time, surely. It's a great rest I'll have now, and great sleeping in the long nights after Samhain, if it's only a bit of wet flour we do have to eat, and maybe a fish that would be stinking.

[*She kneels down again, crossing herself, and saying prayers under her breath.*

*Cathleen* [*to an old man*]. Maybe yourself and Eamon would make a coffin when the sun rises. We have fine white boards herself bought, God help her, thinking Michael would be found, and I have a new cake you can eat while you'll be working.

*The Old Man* [*looking at the boards*]. Are there nails with them?

*Cathleen.* There are not, Colum; we didn't think of the nails.

*Another Man.* It's a great wonder she wouldn't

think of the nails, and all the coffins she's seen made already.

*Cathleen.* It's getting old she is, and broken.

[MAURYA *stands up again very slowly, and spreads out the pieces of* MICHAEL'S *clothes beside the body, sprinkling them with the last of the Holy Water.*

NORA [*in a whisper to* CATHLEEN]. She's quiet now and easy ; but the day Michael was drowned you could hear her crying out from this to the spring well. It's fonder she was of Michael, and would any one have thought that ?

*Cathleen* [*slowly and clearly*]. An old woman will be soon tired with anything she will do, and isn't it nine days herself is after crying and keening, and making great sorrow in the house ?

MAURYA [*puts the empty cup mouth downwards on the table, and lays her hands together on* BARTLEY'S *feet*]. They're all together this time, and the end is come. May the Almighty God have mercy on Bartley's soul, and on Michael's soul, and on the souls of Sheamus and Patch, and Stephen and Shawn [*bending her head*] ; and may He have mercy on my soul, Nora, and on the soul of every one is left living in the world.

[*She pauses, and the keen rises a little more loudly from the women, then sinks away.*

MAURYA [*continuing*]. Michael has a clean burial in the far north, by the grace of the Almighty God. Bartley will have a fine coffin out of the white boards, and a deep grave surely. What more can we want than that ? No man at all can be living for ever, and we must be satisfied.

[*She kneels down again, and the curtain falls slowly.*

# COMMENTARY

## THE ONE-ACT PLAY

THE One-Act Play is regarded by many people as an invention of the twentieth century, but this is only partly true. The short, continuous play, with an approach to artistic unity, is no new thing. It may be one of the oldest forms of drama, for short farcical plays appear to have developed independently in ancient Greece and ancient Italy, and—whether they represent the old tradition or a fresh beginning—short farces flourished in Italy, from the fifteenth to the seventeenth centuries, as the *Commedia dell' arte*, and in other European countries.

The earliest English plays developed, like classical Greek drama, from the ritual of religious worship, and these "mysteries," miracle plays, and interludes of the Middle Ages were nearly all plays in one act.* When the Puritans closed the theatres in 1642, travelling actors who evaded the law often performed short farces called "drolls"; and during the eighteenth and nineteenth centuries many plays in one act were written as "curtain-raisers" or "after-pieces" for the professional theatre, or as the "sketches for amateurs" which are still occasionally inflicted upon us. They were chiefly burlesques or farces, and

* See *Earlier English Drama*, edited by F. J. Tickner, in this Series (No. 55).

represent on the whole a steady degeneration of the one-act form.

Yet, though these and many other instances can be given, it remains unproved that they represent a continuous development, in Europe or in England, of the One-Act Play, for this subject has not been fully investigated. We can be certain only that in the twentieth century the One-Act Play has been re-created—in England and America and many other countries—and recognized for the first time as a distinct dramatic form of high merit, which may be the vehicle of tragedy or comedy, " morality " or fantasy, or almost anything dramatic. Unfortunately there is little demand in our professional theatres for one-act plays, but they are fully appreciated by the " Little Theatres " of America and the steadily advancing amateur dramatic societies of England.

# ON THE PLAYS AND THE AUTHORS

## NORMAN MCKINNEL: THE BISHOP'S CANDLESTICKS

Mr. Norman McKinnel has a high place in the
English theatre of to-day, but as an actor, not as a
dramatist, for he has written only two plays besides this.    The list of the parts he has played
since he began his stage career in 1894 fills three
columns of *Who's Who in the Theatre*, and includes
many well-known characters in plays of Galsworthy,
Shakespeare, and Shaw.    Mr. Frank Vernon, in *The
Twentieth Century Theatre*, has hailed him as " the
typical great actor of the naturalistic school "—the
modern school which does not act *at* the audience, but
ignores it and acts only with and to the other actors
on the stage.    But " it is not method alone, it is the
Herculean figure of the man which makes him so apt a
symbol of the New Drama."

*The Bishop's Candlesticks* is an adaptation of unusual skill.    The story of the encounter of Jean Val-
jean, the convict, with Monseigneur Welcome, Bishop
of D——, occupies Chapters II. to XII. of Book II. of
*Fantine*, in Victor Hugo's novel, *Les Misérables*.    For
this one-act play the long narrative, with its descriptions and retrospections, has been very freely adapted
and compressed.    The play shows no marks of the
process—it might well have been conceived in its
present form; but it keeps the spirit and essence of the
original.

## FOR DISCUSSION

1. For what purpose is the incident of the salt cellars introduced ?

2. What is there unexpected in Persomé's speech beginning " Sorry, and why, pray ? . . . " (page 14). What is her motive in speaking so ?

3. Why does Persomé say, " Brother, brother, you will break my heart " ?

4. Why is the Convict " puzzled " when he repeats, " Suffered, suffered " ?

5. Probably you have noticed that the Bishop is a master of the art of repartee. Which is his most effective reply ?

6. Do you think that the change in the Convict will be permanent ?

7. Is there any weak point in the play ?

## FOR DISCUSSION OR COMPOSITION

8. The danger always with a story like this is that it will become sentimental and unconvincing. Has this happened here, or does the play carry conviction ? Give reasons for your answer.

9. What is the secret of the Bishop's power ?

10. Describe the character of Persomé, and explain the dramatic value of the contrast in character between her and—at opposite extremes—the Bishop and the Convict.

11. Read the chapters of *Les Misérables* on which the play is based, and then explain the purpose of the changes which Mr. McKinnel has made in his dramatization.

12. State in one sentence, and in abstract terms, what you consider to be the theme of the play.

## FURTHER READING

13. Three one-act plays similar to this in theme: *The Only Legend*, by John Drinkwater. *In Safety*, by Margaret Macnamara. *Brother Wolf*, by L. Housman.

## HAROLD CHAPIN : THE PHILOSOPHER OF
## BUTTERBIGGINS

Though Harold Chapin's work belongs entirely to English literature and the English stage, he was an American citizen, born at Brooklyn, U.S.A., in 1886. His mother, an American actress, brought him to England when he was two years old ; at the age of seven he appeared as young Marcus in Shakespeare's *Coriolanus*, at Stratford-on-Avon, and his first attempt at playwriting was made a few months later !

In 1902 he went on the stage in earnest, and acted in some queer plays with travelling companies before his engagement for a Drury Lane pantomime. Thereafter he played many parts in London and Glasgow, he studied music, and wrote a good deal of poetry, but it was as producer and dramatist that he won distinction. His persistent ambition was to write plays, and in this he was well served by his insatiable interest in life, " his keen sense of humour and delight in every living thing from a bumble bee to a bad actor," and his abounding vitality.

His apparently instinctive appreciation of dramatic technique, which must have been fostered by his early apprenticeship to the stage, was as true as his sense of the " right word " and his command of dialogue. The one-act plays which are the best of his work deal, for the most part, with the life of very poor people, whom he portrayed with clear, critical sympathy and understanding, without bias or sentimentality.

His first play, *Augustus in Search of a Father*, was produced at the Court Theatre in 1910, and in the next four years he wrote sixteen plays—ten of them one-act. But his work was only just beginning when the Great War broke out. He joined the R.A.M.C. in September 1914 ; he was killed in the Battle of Loos on September 26, 1915, while bringing in wounded under fire.

It is impossible not to feel that by his death, at the age of twenty-nine, our drama lost a great deal, as poetry lost by the death of Rupert Brooke. We are reminded once again how tragically war secures not the survival, but the destruction, of the fittest.

## FOR DISCUSSION

People with a keen sense of humour have every right to be solemn, and perhaps they are the only people who have any right at all. If we have enjoyed the light-hearted comedy of *The Philosopher*, we can give the following portentous questions our earnest attention :

14. Good titles are hard to find, but *The Philosopher of Butterbiggins* is particularly well chosen, and difficult to forget. Why ?

15. What are the arguments for and against such detailed descriptions of the setting, and the characters, as Chapin gives at the beginning of this play ?

16. Which is Lizzie's most illogical remark, and which shows most clearly her kindness of heart ?

17. What other plays or stories do you know which derive a distinctive richness of humour from their Scottish dialect and characters ?

## FOR DISCUSSION OR COMPOSITION

18. Arrange Lizzie, John, and David—first in order of intelligence, and second in order of strength of purpose, and justify the arrangements.

19. Is the humour of the play provided more by the characterization or by the plot ?

20. Look up " philosopher " in a good dictionary, and then try to decide whether David is right in calling himself a philosopher.

21. Write the " story o' the kelpies up at Crosshill wi' the tram." If you know the language of Scotland well (not otherwise), write it as David would tell it. (Kelpies are mischievous spirits said to haunt fords and ferries at night, especially during storms.)

## FURTHER READING

22. *Augustus in Search of a Father*, *It's the Poor that helps the Poor*, and *The Autocrat of the Coffee Stall*, one-act plays by Harold Chapin.

23. Stories of Scottish life and character : *A Window in Thrums* and *Sentimental Tommy*, novels by J. M. Barrie. *Wee Macgreegor*, by J. J. Bell. *The Glen is Mine*, a play by John Brandane.

## Maurice Baring : The Rehearsal

During his varied career in the Diplomatic Service and the Royal Air Force the Honourable Maurice Baring has written poems, plays, novels, and critical essays, including a number of essays on Russian literature.

His volume of *Diminutive Dramas*, from which *The Rehearsal* is taken, consists of little one-act plays which appeared originally in the *Morning Post*. Nearly all of them deal lightly with famous characters and incidents—King Alfred and the cakes, for instance ; a dinner-party given by Julius Cæsar's wife, Calpurnia ; and Henry VIII. quarrelling with Catherine Parr at breakfast. Like this play, they are marked by a lively wit and ingenuity, and depend for humorous effect chiefly upon a general lowering of the emotional level, so that characters whom we expect to be heroic appear as very ordinary people. Medea, for example, instead of being a terrible enchantress, is a hostess worried as to whom she should ask to dinner !

*The Rehearsal* presents an imaginary situation such as *might* have inspired Shakespeare's famous lines, " To-morrow, and to-morrow, and to-morrow . . ."

Shakespeare's biographers have patiently collected a mass of details concerning his outward life, but very little is known of the man himself. Except in so far as it is revealed in his plays, we know less of his personality than we do of his income, and since his work has been read and loved and studied more than that of any other English writer, it is inevitable that stories and plays should be written about him. In some of these he is introduced simply to lend romance or historical interest ; others, such as Miss Clemence Dane's poetic tragedy, *Will Shakespeare*, attempt an imaginative reconstruction of his character.

## FOR DISCUSSION

24. Read the fifth act of *Macbeth*. This will greatly increase your appreciation of *The Rehearsal*.

25. The author has dealt freely with characterization and several other points in the play. The Globe Theatre had no " wings " in the modern sense ; the actors entered by doors on either side of the stage. The Producer and Stage Manager were not given those titles. Richard Burbage, a friend of the dramatist, was the great tragedian who played Richard III., Hamlet, Othello, and other leading Shakespearean rôles. Shakespeare himself is traditionally reputed not to have been a very good actor, and to have played such parts as the Ghost in *Hamlet*, and Adam in *As You Like It*.

Choose two adjectives to describe the character given to each of the following in the play : Shakespeare, Burbage, and the Producer.

26. What is the meaning of the terms " bathos," " burlesque," and " farce " ? Illustrate them from the play.

27. What was a masque ? What famous entertainment was given to Queen Elizabeth at Kenilworth, and where is it described ?

28. The point of the reference to Mistress Mary Fytton is that, after many attempts by critics to identify her with the " dark lady " of Shakespeare's Sonnets, it has now been shown that she was fair. What was the colour of Queen Elizabeth's hair ?

29. What difference do you imagine in the tones of the actors' voices when they are rehearsing their parts in

*Macbeth* and when they are talking in their own characters ?

30. Study Mr. Gordon Craig's illustration for the lines " To-morrow, and to-morrow, and to-morrow . . ." in his book *On the Art of the Theatre*. What do you think of it ?

## FOR DISCUSSION OR COMPOSITION

31. How does this play differ from most " historical " plays ?

32. What do you think of Burbage's couplet, O dearest chuck, etc., and his suggestion that a speech in rhyme should be added in Act V., Scene v. ?

33. Write a little story or play about any historical incident with which you are familiar, in the manner of *The Rehearsal*.

## FURTHER READING

34. *Diminutive Dramas* (especially Nos. 1, 5, 8, and 18), by Maurice Baring.

35. *Shakespeare's Christmas*, by Sir A. T. Quiller-Couch (" Q "), a short story of the building of the Globe Theatre. *Will Shakespeare*, by Clemence Dane.

## HAROLD BRIGHOUSE : THE PRICE OF COAL

The work of Mr. Brighouse is closely identified with the Gaiety Theatre, Manchester, which Miss A. E. F. Horniman opened in the autumn of 1907, with the avowed purpose of making it " a repertory theatre *

---

* A repertory theatre is a theatre with a permanent company of actors who have a repertoire of plays. They do not give a large number of *consecutive* performances of any play, however popular it may be, but change their " bill " very frequently (sometimes two or three times a week), and revive old plays as well as produce new ones. Usually the plays are chosen with rather more regard for artistic values than for probability of financial success. The " long-run " system of the ordinary commercial theatre has obvious financial advantages, but it is artistically very bad for both dramatist and actor.

with a regular change of programme, not wedded to any one school of dramatists but thoroughly catholic, embracing the finest writing of the best authors of all ages, and with an especially widely open door to present-day British writers." The work of this famous theatre, and of the repertory theatres of Dublin, Glasgow, Liverpool, Birmingham, and London, marks an epoch in the history of our drama, and did much towards rescuing it from the complete domination of the " commercial " theatre.

Miss Horniman's splendid work at Manchester gave an incentive and an opportunity to a number of local dramatists—Stanley Houghton, Mr. Allan Monk-house, Mr. Harold Brighouse, Mr. Charles McEvoy, and others. They all wrote realistic plays of present-day life, but did not limit themselves to Lancashire settings, and the term " Manchester School," which is sometimes applied to them, is misleading.

Mr. Brighouse was educated at Manchester Grammar School, where Houghton and Mr. Gilbert Cannan were among his schoolfellows. He began writing plays about the time he left school to enter the cotton trade—which he did not altogether abandon for literature until 1915. After some years of unsuccessful dramatic writing, he had *The Doorway* and other plays produced in 1909 ; since that date more than twenty of his plays have been staged—of which *Hobson's Choice* and *Garside's Career* have probably been the most popular. None of his later one-act plays, however, has surpassed *The Price of Coal*, written in 1909. It has all the qualities of his best work—accurate and sympathetic observation of character, convincing realism, and tense drama woven from the everyday lives of " commonplace " people.

## FOR DISCUSSION

36. Does the play gain by being written in dialect ?
If so, in what way ?

37. What is the effect upon the reader of Ellen's talk
about her dream ?  Can you suggest any other way in
which a similar effect could be obtained ?

38. What are the chief differences between Mary and
Ellen, and to what are they partly due ?

39. What does the title imply ?

## FOR DISCUSSION OR COMPOSITION

40. Show how far the play bears out the description
of the miners and their womenfolk which the author
gives in his opening stage directions.

41. Did you expect Jack to be killed ?  Would the
play be strengthened if he were ?

42. Write an essay on " Dangerous Trades," or " The
Price of Comfort," or " Modern Industrial Types."

43. Write a short story or a one-act play about some
occupation in which you are especially interested.

## FURTHER READING

44. *Followers* and *Lonesome Like,* one-act plays by
Harold Brighouse.

45. *Snug in my Easy-Chair,* by W. W. Gibson (in *Poems
of To-day,* Second Series).

## BEULAH MARIE DIX : ALLISON'S LAD

Miss Dix is an American dramatist—her ancestors
were among the original settlers in Massachusetts—
but she has spent a good deal of time in England, and
many of her plays and novels are English in subject.
She has written much since her first play, *Cicely's
Cavalier,* was acted in the college theatre during her

undergraduate days at Harvard.    In this country her best-known play is *The Breed of the Treshams*, which she wrote in collaboration with Evelyn Greenleaf Sutherland, under the pen-name of " John Rutherford."    This was first produced in England in 1903 by Sir John Martin-Harvey, and he played in it for a number of years.    In America her best-known plays are probably *The Road to Yesterday* and *Across the Border*.

Her novels include *The Fighting Blade, Hugh Gwyeth, Blount of Breckenhow*, and *The Fair Maid of Graystones*, all stories of the time of Cromwell; and *The Gate of Horn*, a tale of Cornwall in the present day.

For the past ten years she has written almost exclusively for the cinema, and has lived in Hollywood, " in a brown Californian cottage, with roses in the garden, and dogs under foot."

## FOR DISCUSSION

46. In what way does the speech of Winwood, Goring, and Hopton differ from that of the other characters ?

47. What is suggested by Winwood's remark, " You called me, Sir ? " and Strickland's reply ?    What peculiar importance has this suggestion with regard to the climax of the play ?    What other similar suggestions can you find ?

48. There are two verbal repetitions in the play which are very effective.    What are they, and why are they effective ?

49. Why does Strickland harp on the idea that Winwood is a gallant lad ?

50. In what way does the dramatist prepare us for the revelation that Winwood has broken his parole, and that Goring and Hopton have done so ?    In which case is the preparation more elaborate, and why ?    How does this preparation strengthen the play ?

51. Why does Bowyer say " In good time, Colonel Drummond ! " when the latter enters ?

52. What feelings is Bowyer expressing when he says, " Frank Hopton, too ? "

53. What do you think of the defence made by the three who have broken their paroles ?

54. " I'm a coward," says Tom Winwood. Is this true ?

55. Whose was the " strong arm " that was round Winwood at the last ?

56. How does Strickland learn that " Allison's lad " died gallantly ?

57. In what way has the dramatist prepared the audience for Strickland's death ?

58. Where does the climax of this play occur ?

## FOR DISCUSSION OR COMPOSITION

59. " The three at table talk heatedly in dumb-show." Describe this dumb-show in detail, taking care to make the actions of each man as characteristic of him as possible.

60. Write a character sketch of Tom Winwood, or Strickland, or Allison.

61. Is the play strengthened or weakened by the supernatural element at the end ? Can you suggest another ending, without this element, which would be as good ?

62. If you examine the play carefully you will find that it can be divided naturally into sections, just as a short story is divided into paragraphs. For instance, it is obvious that the second section begins with Bowyer's question, " How is it with you, Will, old lad ? "

Make these divisions, and write down the first line of each and a short title for each. You can learn from this a good deal about the structure of the play.

63. You will sometimes see the term " Wardour Street English " used in connection with historical novels and plays. It is derived from the name of a London street which was famous for its dealers in antique and pseudo-antique furniture, and it is used to describe the archaic style which some writers adopt to give their stories an atmosphere of the past. Used clumsily, this method soon becomes absurd : we quickly tire of the robber baron, however bad he may be, who always calls his

servant " varlet," and garnishes every speech with such
words as " anent " and " erst " and " by my halidom ! "
What do you think of Miss Dix's archaisms ?

## FURTHER READING

64. *Campbell of Kilmhor*, by J. A. Ferguson.  $X=O$,
by John Drinkwater.  *In Safety*, by Margaret Macnamara.  (Three one-act plays dealing with episodes in
various wars.)

## Bernard Gilbert : The Old Bull

Two writers of our time have devoted themselves,
with remarkable success, to areas of the English
countryside which they know and love.  Mr. Thomas
Hardy, who is by common consent our greatest living
novelist, has re-created in his " Wessex " novels and
tales the whole life of the western and south-western
counties, in town and village and farm.  Miss Sheila
Kaye Smith has followed suit with her novels of
Sussex.  Now, on a different plane, Mr. Bernard
Gilbert has set out to give us his view of the rural
scene, but instead of describing actual places thinly
disguised, he has invented " Bly District," " a section
of three or four hundred square miles, offered as an
example of rural England, uncontaminated by English
civilization. . . . Reference to the map shows it running up from the sea, through successive belts of
marsh, fen, sand, heath, moor, and limestone, embracing most kinds of soil and methods of cultivation,
and nearly all classes of countrymen."

Indeed, Mr. Gilbert seems to have taken very liter-
ally R. L. Stevenson's advice * to writers to study the
map, real or imaginary, of the scene of their stories :
his books are equipped not only with maps and plans,

---

* See *My First Book*.  It is in the edition of *Treasure Island*
in this Series.

but with directories and family trees ! Whatever may be said of this apparatus of realism, Mr. Gilbert's thirty years' observation of rural life gives truth to his characters and stories, and, like most modern writers, he does not write us pretty conventional descriptions of " Sweet Auburn, loveliest village of the plain," as it appears to the casual visitor from the town ; he depicts villages as he sees them at close quarters.

*The Old Bull* is one of several plays which appear in the volume entitled *King Lear at Hordle*. It is not one of the author's most serious studies of rural life, but it is a pleasant comedy which plays very well, and Tom Bones, at least, deserves our attention. He is still to be found in the lonelier English farms. His repetitions, his devotion to his bull, his stubborn adherence to the one idea, are not mere stage tricks, but characteristics of his class. We should try to appreciate him, for with the present rapid development of the small motor-omnibus he and his like will soon cease to exist.

## FOR DISCUSSION

65. In what way would the Elmitts have learned the value of their furniture, " if Pantacks were not down in the Gulland marshes " ?

66. Is the explanation of the state of affairs at the beginning of the play made natural and interesting ?

67. Which is Charles's most unpleasant remark ?

68. A dramatist often prepares the way for an important incident or disclosure by giving hints and suggestions, which make it more convincing when it comes. In this play, how are we prepared for the disclosure of the will and its terms, and for the death of Brutus ?

69. When is Bones most amusing ?

70. What is the meaning of the phrases " poetic justice " and " hoist with his own petard " ? Who was the author of the latter ? How do they apply to this play ?

## FOR DISCUSSION OR COMPOSITION

71. Is the title of the play well chosen ?

72. Re-read the description of the Grange kitchen, visualizing it as clearly as you can, and then describe the best bedroom and the view from one of its windows.

73. Does the death of the old bull make the ending of the play seem artificially neat ?   Did you anticipate it ? If so, at what point in the play, and why ?

74. Write a short monologue in which Charles gives a friend his version of the incidents of the play.   (To do this well you must not only imitate his manner of speech, but realize clearly how things appear to him and how he will try to justify himself.)

## FURTHER READING

75. *King Lear at Hordle* and *To Arms !*, by Bernard Gilbert.   (Both plays are in the volume which bears the title of the former.)

76. *Under the Greenwood Tree*, by Thomas Hardy. Poems by Thomas Hardy and Edmund Blunden in *Methuen's Anthology of Modern Verse* and *Poems of To-day*.

## John Galsworthy : The Little Man

Of the four outstanding dramatists of our time, Mr. George Bernard Shaw, Sir James Barrie, Mr John Galsworthy, and J. M. Synge, the first does not appear in this book because his one-act plays do not adequately represent his expansive genius, and the second purely for reasons of copyright.   The last two writers, however, are well represented by *The Little Man* and *Riders to the Sea*.

Mr. John Galsworthy was educated at Harrow and Oxford, and then—like a number of other English writers—he studied law, and was called to the Bar in 1890.   But he found his profession very distasteful, and probably it is more from temperament than from legal training that his work derives the restrained impartiality, the care in stating both sides of a case, for which he is famous.    When he turned to literature it was first to write novels and stories.    His *Forsyte Saga*, a series of novels dealing with the fortunes of an English family, is one of the notable achievements of contemporary fiction, and it is also popular.

His first play, *The Silver Box*, was produced at the Court Theatre in 1906 under the Vedrenne-Barker management, which, with the Repertory movement, did so much to bring literature and drama together again.    Mr. Galsworthy has never surpassed *The Silver Box*, but he has equalled it in several of the plays, over twenty in number, which he has written since, and of which *Joy, Strife, Justice, The Pigeon, The Mob,* and *Loyalties* are the best.    They are all seriously concerned with some fundamental problem of our social life, such as the clash between " capital " and " labour," and they state the problem with the full force of the dramatist's mastery of natural dialogue, exciting stage-effect, and stern realism of detail. They are gigantic question marks, and they leave it to the audience to seek the answer.    They are not the stuff of which popular successes are usually made, but several of them have been very popular successes— because they are such good stage-plays.

## FOR DISCUSSION

77. From what has been said above about Mr. Galsworthy's work, would you regard this play as entirely characteristic of him ?

78. The author describes the play as a " farcical morality."    In what way is it farcical ?    (The keynote of farce is theatrical exaggeration for the sake of humorous effect.)

79. Why are the characters described only by their nationality, and not by their personal names ?

80. Why are there so many more characters in this play than in the other plays in this book ?

81. Are any of these characters superfluous ?

82. Is the author fair to them all, or does his famous impartiality not appear in this play ?

83. In what is the Little Man different from all the other characters ?

84. Has the author stated a problem in this play ? If so, what is it ?

85. If a problem is stated, has the author left it to the audience to find a solution, or has he, in this case, offered a solution ?

86. What is the Little Man's nationality ?

87. What connection is there between this play and the idea of the League of Nations ?

88. If the play is a morality, what is the moral ?

### FOR DISCUSSION OR COMPOSITION

89. State the theme of the play in one sentence and in abstract terms.

90. Re-write the play as a short story.

91. Compare your story with Mr. Galsworthy's story of *The Little Man ;* or read his instead of writing your own, and then describe, and comment upon, the differences between story and play. (*The Little Man* appears as a story in *Caravan*, 7s. 6d., and in a smaller volume at 2s.)

### FURTHER READING

92. *Strife* (a play), *The Forsyte Saga* (novels), and *Caravan* (collected short stories), by John Galsworthy.

### CLIFFORD BAX : THE POETASTERS OF ISPAHAN

Mr. Clifford Bax published in 1925 a volume of reminiscences of unusual charm, entitled *Inland Far.* He describes his boyhood at Hampstead, in the days when it was more a village than a suburb ; his wanderings round the world ; his meetings with poets, musicians, and artists ; and those adventures of mind and spirit which count for so much more in a man's life than the dates and facts which usually constitute a " short biography."

The title *Inland Far*, quoted from Wordsworth's *Ode on the Intimations of Immortality*, suggests the quality of much of Mr. Bax's work. It includes mystical poetry and paraphrases of Chinese poems, besides a number of plays in rhymed verse which blend fantasy and light satire with farcical comedy. His latest play, *Mr. Pepys*, is a ballad-opera in the eighteenth-century manner, with prose dialogue and many songs.

Of Mr. Bax's one-act plays *The Poetasters of Ispahan* is undoubtedly the best, and it is even better to act than to read.

## FOR DISCUSSION

93. Could *The Poetasters* have been written just as well in blank verse or prose ? What other plays do you know which are written in rhyme ?

94. At what point does the play reach its crisis ?

95. Do you take it for granted, almost from the beginning, that Hallaj will win Silvermoon ? If so, what maintains your interest in the play ?

96. Which passages of the verse appeal to you most ?

97. Why should Suliman be given " something fair and fine " ?

## FOR DISCUSSION OR COMPOSITION

98. What are the advantages and disadvantages of a character's addressing the audience at the beginning of a play, as Hallaj does here ? Do you like it ? Does it strike the keynote of this play ?

99. By what characteristic phrases do the suitors show the trades to which they belong ?

100. Write another quatrain to Silvermoon.

101. Write a short epilogue in rhyme for a performance of this play by your own school or society.

## FURTHER READING

102. *Old King Cole* and *Square Pegs*, by Clifford Bax.
103. *Tales from " The Arabian Nights "* in this Series
(T.E.S. 16).


## J. M. Synge : Riders to the Sea

It was in 1899 that the Irish Literary Theatre was
founded in Dublin by Mr. W. B. Yeats, Lady Gregory,
and others, as an amateur society which struggled on
until the generosity of Miss Horniman established it at
the Abbey Theatre, Dublin, in 1904.

The theatre became a school of dramatists and of
players who have attained a world-wide reputation ;
their work is the most important phase of the Irish
literary revival, which began towards the end of last
century, and was in part political as well as literary—
an outcome of the national desire for independence.

John Millington Synge was brought into the company of the Abbey Theatre by Mr. W. B. Yeats.
Synge was born near Dublin in 1871, graduated at
Trinity College, Dublin, in 1892, and then—rather like
Oliver Goldsmith—wandered with his violin through
France and Germany. Mr. Yeats found him in Paris,
trying to make a living by literary journalism, and
persuaded him to return to Ireland in 1898. There
for some years he lived among the peasants, and his
genius, which had wilted in the hothouse atmosphere
of Paris, grew and flourished among the hills and
islands. But his health failed. He died of cancer in
1909, when his work had just begun. Yet though he
has left us only six plays he is recognized as the one
great dramatist of the Irish theatre, and held by
many to be the greatest dramatist, except Shakespeare, who has ever written in the English tongue.

Synge found the characters and the ideas for his

plays among the Irish peasants and fisherfolk with whom he lived in the Aran Islands, in Kerry and Wicklow and Connemara. Their primitive life, their struggle with the relentless forces of Nature, their brutality and passion and boisterous humour, provided him with the material for comedies and tragedies which are unique in English, while his genius gave them universal significance and appeal. The subtle characterization, the strange setting, and the fine technique of Synge's plays are no more striking than the peculiar language in which they are written. Synge was one of the artists, all too few, who can write wisely and briefly upon their own art. In his preface to *The Playboy of the Western World* he says : " I have used one or two words only that I have not heard among the country people of Ireland, or spoken in my own nursery before I could read the newspapers. A certain number of the phrases I employ I have heard also from herds and fishermen along the coast from Kerry to Mayo, or from beggar-women or balladsingers nearer Dublin, and I am glad to acknowledge how much I owe to the folk imagination of these fine people. . . . All art is a collaboration, and there is little doubt that in the happy ages of literature striking and beautiful phrases were as ready to the story-teller's or the playwright's hand as the rich cloaks and dresses of his time. . . . On the stage one must have reality and one must have joy ; and that is why the intellectual modern drama has failed, and people have grown sick of the false joy of the musical comedy that has been given them in place of the rich joy found only in what is superb and wild in reality. In a good play every speech should be as fully flavoured as a nut or apple, and such speeches cannot be written by any one who works among people who have shut their lips on poetry. . . ."

From this popular speech—a dialect of English enriched by Celtic turns of phrase and thought—Synge wove the highly artificial prose of his plays, cadenced and beautiful, full of poetry, and a fit vehicle for his highest tragedy and richest humour.

*Riders to the Sea* (1904), his greatest one-act play, is also his greatest tragedy. Its combination of mysticism and realism, and its height of emotion, make it truly representative of Irish drama and of the genius of Synge.

## FOR DISCUSSION

104. This play deals with poor people who are living under peculiar local conditions, remote from civilization. What gives it " universal significance and appeal " ?

105. Is there any amount of deep *pathos* in the play ?

106. Read what is said about conflict in Section 113. What is the conflict here ?

107. To represent J. M. Synge in *The Oxford Book of English Prose*, Sir Arthur Quiller-Couch has chosen an extract from *Riders to the Sea*, equal to about a page of this book. Which extract would you choose, and why ?

## FOR DISCUSSION OR COMPOSITION

108. From consideration of this play evolve a definition of tragedy which does not include the idea of death.

109. Compare Maurya with Ellen in *The Price of Coal*, and say which is the greater character, and why.

110. Why is *Riders to the Sea* put last in this book ?

## FURTHER READING

111. The plays of J. M. Synge, especially *The Playboy of the Western World* and *Deirdre of the Sorrows*. (The six plays are published in one volume at 6s. 6d. by Messrs. Allen and Unwin.)

112. *Plays and Controversies*, by W. B. Yeats. *Seven Short Plays* and *Our Irish Theatre*, by Lady Augusta Gregory. *J. M. Synge* (in *Recent Prose*), by John Masefield.

# GENERAL EXERCISES ON DRAMA AND DRAMATIC COMPOSITION

113. The very essence of drama is conflict, and this may be of two different kinds—outer, and inner, conflict. Outer conflict takes place between two men or groups of men, or between a man and the society about him, or a power above him such as " fate " : we have such a conflict between Cæsar's party and Brutus's party in *Julius Cæsar*, and between Hamlet and his uncle ; between Malvolio and Sir Toby's party in *Twelfth Night*, and between Falstaff and society in general in *Henry IV*.

Inner conflict takes place in a character's nature. Sometimes it is between emotions which outward circumstances cause to clash, such as the struggle in the mind of Brutus between his patriotism and his love for Cæsar, or the struggle in Macbeth between ambition and honour. The general tendency of both tragedy and comedy, from the time of the ancient Greeks to our own day, has been to give more and more attention to the inner, and less to the outer, conflict. Many plays contain both types, and these, of which *Hamlet* is the supreme example, are most likely to be both successful stage-plays and masterpieces of literature, because the outer conflict is easier to represent on the stage and holds the attention of the audience more firmly, while the inner conflict is more permanently interesting, more profound and satisfying.

Which plays in this volume are based chiefly upon (*a*) outer, and (*b*) inner conflict, and which upon the two combined ?

114. Our interest in dramatic conflict is greatly increased when we are kept in suspense as to the result (which does not necessarily mean that we are ignorant of the result), and so dramatists sometimes deliberately create suspense.

Find instances of this in comedy and in tragedy in this book.

115. It has been well said that a play can never rise above the level of its characterization. Though we may enjoy them thoroughly at the time, we feel that farce and melodrama, *Charley's Aunt* and *Bull-dog Drummond*, are inferior to comedy and tragedy because for their effects they depend upon theatrical incidents, upon transient things, and to gain these they sacrifice truth—especially truth and depth of characterization. They have no real connection with life. The difficulty of depicting characters in a short play must be one reason why the one-act play was almost limited to farce for so long.

116. Here are some critical opinions which are well worth pondering and discussing :

" Tragedy is the imitation of one entire, great, and probable action, not told, but represented, which, by moving in us fear and pity, is conducive to the purging of those two passions in our mind."—Aristotle, *Poetics* (*c.* 330 B.C.).

This famous theory of the " catharsis " (purging) by tragedy has been discussed more than anything else ever written about drama : it must certainly not be accepted without discussion. Why is high tragedy never depressing ? What kind of pleasure does it give ?

117. " The test of true comedy is that it shall awaken thoughtful laughter. . . . The stroke of the great humorist is world wide."—George Meredith, *An Essay on Comedy* (1897).

" Tragedy at its best is a vision of the heart of life. The heart of life can only be laid bare in the agony and exultation of dreadful acts. The vision of agony, or spiritual contest, pushed beyond the limits of the dying personality, is exulting and cleansing. It is only by such vision that a multitude can be brought to the passionate knowledge of things exalting and eternal."— John Masefield, Preface to *The Tragedy of Nan* (1908).

" The drama is made serious—in the French sense of the word—not by the degree in which it is taken up with problems that are serious in themselves, but by the

degree in which it gives the nourishment, not very easy
to define, on which our imaginations live.   We should
not go to the theatre as we go to a chemist's, or a dram-
shop, but as we go to a dinner where the food we need is
taken with pleasure and excitement. . . . Of the things
which nourish the imagination humour is one of the most
needful, and it is dangerous to limit or destroy it."—
J. M. Synge, Preface to *The Tinker's Wedding* (1907).

" The nourishment . . . on which our imaginations
live . . . taken with pleasure and excitement."   There
is much food for thought here.

Do you think that any of the tragedies and comedies
in this book satisfy the requirements of Meredith and
Masefield and Synge ?   If so, which are they ?   And
which are the failures ?

Meredith was a novelist and Synge a dramatist, and
Mr. Masefield is both.

118. Mr. H. W. Fowler has recently published a
*Dictionary of Modern English Usage* (Oxford University
Press, 7s. 6d.) which should be within reach of every one
who is writing or trying to write.   If you can get hold of
the book, study the illuminating article on " humour,
wit, satire, sarcasm, invective, irony, cynicism, the
sardonic," and illustrate each of these terms with
examples from the plays in this collection.

119. " The primary magic of the theatre is the spoken
word."—Frank Vernon.   What do you think of this ?

120. What advantages has the cinema over the theatre,
and vice versa ?   What are the chief defects of the usual
cinema entertainment ?

121. It seems very probable that in a few years' time
broadcast wireless television will be as fully developed
as wireless telephony is at present.   Do you think that
the combination of the two is likely to supersede the
theatre altogether ?   What advantages has the theatre ?

122. Write a short criticism of any modern play which
you have seen performed recently.   (Deal with the play,
the acting, and the stage-settings, and remember that
criticism involves appreciation of the good as well as the
bad points.)

123. Who were the authors of the following plays ?
*The Alchemist, The Admirable Crichton, The Good-*

*natured Man, The Critic, The Silver Box, The Knight of the Burning Pestle, The Conquering Hero, The Twelve-Pound Look, The Two Gentlemen of Verona, The Frogs, The Trojan Women, The Wild Duck, The Miser, The Rising of the Moon, The Dear Departed, The Winter's Tale, The Land of Heart's Desire, The Devil's Disciple, The Importance of Being Earnest, The Tragedy of Nan, The Cenci, The Plough and the Stars, The Blue Bird, The Rivals, The Shoemakers' Holiday.*

124. Write down the titles and the authors of the plays in which the following characters appear :

Autolycus, Lydia Languish, Old Gobbo, Felix Drinkwater, Justice Shallow, Mrs. Malaprop, Mistress Merrythought, Pegeen Mike, Horatio, Iago, Queen Dollalolla, Campaspe, Puff, Ophelia, Bobadilla, Tony Lumpkin, Tom Winwood, Hecuba, Tyltyl, Sir Harry Sims, Sir Peter Teazle, Sir Andrew Aguecheek, Sir Howard Hallam, Sir John Falstaff, Britannicus, Lord Loam, Brother Juniper.

125. Which plays in this book would you choose as most suitable for performance (1) at your school speech-day, (2) at a school concert, given at the end of the Christmas term, (3) by Form IV., (4) by a Scout Troop, (5) by an O.T.C., and (6) by a branch of the League of Nations Union ? Give two plays for (6), and one for each of the others, explaining the reasons for your choice in each case.

126. Draw up from this book a programme of two, three, or four plays (according to the number of actors available) for performance by your own form or society. Choose and arrange the plays carefully, to give the programme artistic harmony and unity, which is not very easily done. Then cast the plays, giving every person available the part for which he or she is most suited, omitting no one, and in a very few cases giving two parts to one player if this proves necessary. A play which cannot be cast fairly well should not be put in the programme.

127. When you have drawn up this programme of plays, write a short prologue for it, in rhymed verse.

128. Which part would you choose for yourself in your programme, and why ?

129. In Browning's *Fra Lippo Lippi*, the friar-painter says, in defence of his art :

" For, don't you mark, we're made so that we love
First when we see them painted, things we have passed
Perhaps a hundred times nor cared to see ;
And so they are better, painted—better to us,
Which is the same thing.    Art was given for that—
God uses us to help each other so,
Lending our minds out.''

130. Is there any play in this book which has made you feel that this may well be applied to drama, with " men and women " instead of " things " ?

131. Which plays in this book would you describe as " realistic " and which as " poetic " ?    Discuss the meaning of the terms before you decide, and remember that a play need not be written in verse to be poetic in spirit.

132. A reviewer said recently that a play contained much realism and very little reality.    What did he mean ?

133. The majority of modern plays deal with the life of the present day, and many with poor people.    Do you prefer these to historical plays ?    What are the advantages and disadvantages (a) for tragedy, (b) for comedy, in choosing as the chief characters of a play Irish fishermen or London costers, instead of emperors and queens and nobles of the " storied past " ?

134. It used to be regarded as essential to great tragedy that the protagonists should be of high rank, on the ground that their misfortunes and their fall would excite deeper compassion and were worthier subjects for drama.    Do you agree with this, or do you think that a great tragedy can be written about people of humble position ?    Consider the tragic plays which you know.

## A SHORT LIST OF MODERN PLAYS

Recommended for schools and reading circles
(One-act plays are marked *)

GEORGE BERNARD SHAW : *Saint Joan ; Major Barbara, Captain Brassbound's Conversion ; The Devil's Disciple ; Cæsar and Cleopatra*.    (The last three are in " Plays for Puritans.")

JOHN GALSWORTHY : *Strife ; Loyalties*.

SIR JAMES M. BARRIE : *The Admirable Crichton ; The Twelve-Pound Look* * *; The Will* * *; The Old Lady shows her Medals.* *

JOHN MASEFIELD : *The Tragedy of Nan.*

JOHN DRINKWATER : *Abraham Lincoln ; Oliver Cromwell ; X=0, A Night of the Trojan War.* *

GORDON BOTTOMLEY : *Midsummer Eve.*

J. M. SYNGE : *The Playboy of the Western World ; Deirdre of the Sorrows.*

W. B. YEATS : *Cathleen ni Houlihan* * *; The Land of Heart's Desire* * *; The Countess Cathleen.*

LADY GREGORY : *Seven Short Plays.* *

LORD DUNSANY : *The Gods of the Mountain ; The Golden Doom* * *; A Night at an Inn* * *; The Laughter of the Gods.*

LAURENCE HOUSMAN : *Little Plays of St. Francis.* *

## SOME BOOKS ON MODERN DRAMA

*A Study of the Modern Drama.* Barrett H. Clark. Appleton and Co. 15s.

This valuable book, an encyclopedia of facts and critical ideas, is particularly suitable for the school library and for reading circles, because it suggests lines of thought rather than offers definite conclusions. Half the book is given to English, Irish, and American drama ; the other half to the drama of Norway, Russia, France, and other European countries. Exceptionally useful bibliographies and index.

*The Twentieth Century Theatre.* Frank Vernon. Harrap. 5s.

The best short book on the subject, by a writer with first-hand knowledge, and a forceful and witty style.

*Tendencies of Modern English Drama.* A. E. Morgan. Constable. 12s. 6d.

From the Early Victorians to 1923, with detailed criticism of the work of the leading dramatists.

*On the Art of the Theatre.* Edward Gordon Craig. Heinemann. 10s. 6d.

One of the most stimulating, provocative, and original books ever written about acting, production, and stage design.

# ON WRITING ONE-ACT PLAYS

135. The form of drama with which we are most concerned in this book, the One-Act Play, is as distinct from the long play as the short story is from the novel. The difference is not merely one of length ; a true one-act play is not a condensed three-act play, nor can it be elaborated into a three-act play. The difference is not in continuity of action. The difference is a question of structure and of nature. A one-act play deals with a single dominant dramatic situation, and aims at producing a single effect, though the method used may vary greatly, from tragedy to farce, according to the nature of the effect desired. And since the play is to be acted in a short space of time, the greatest artistic unity and economy are essential to success. The attention of the audience must be seized at once and held to the end. There is *no time* for weak exposition, or dull or superfluous speeches, or a divided aim, because the play is too short to recover from any such defect—as a long play will sometimes recover. The one-act play demands the most scrupulous attention to structure and dialogue, and its artistic possibilities are almost unlimited.

Is *The Little Man* a one-act play ? Would *Allison's Lad* or *The Old Bull* gain by being expanded into a long play in several acts ?

136. Having enjoyed the plays in this book, you may like to try your hand as a playwright. To write really good plays demands literary ability of a special kind, and a first-hand knowledge of stage conditions, so you need not be surprised if your first essay is not a masterpiece, but the attempt is well worth making, and as fascinating as it is profitable. You may prefer to begin work on your play without more ado, following your own methods, but if your aim is to produce a play good enough for perform-

ance by your own school or society, a few preliminary suggestions and exercises may be serviceable.

137. First, as to the material. If you can take this from the life around you, and create plot and characters of your own, so much the better. Accurate observation is the basis of good writing, especially dramatic writing, and you will almost certainly write best about the things which you know best. Everyday life is full of suggestions for plays—to those who know how to use them—though it may be necessary to warn a beginner of the danger of trying to put on the stage the incredible people and improbable events which are not at all uncommon in real life !

138. If you prefer a historical subject—and there is a great deal to be said for the costume play, especially where young actors are concerned—then choose and study carefully an episode which appeals to you, say from the history of your own school or town, or from the life of some great man of the past. In this connection you cannot do better than study Mr. John Drinkwater's methods in his fine chronicle plays, *Abraham Lincoln* and *Oliver Cromwell*, or Shakespeare's in *Julius Cæsar*. (The edition of *Julius Cæsar* in this series contains all the extracts from Plutarch's *Lives* which Shakespeare used, so that you can see exactly what he did with his material.) When a number of writers are to work together on a long play, the chronicle-play is the best type to choose, because they can write a scene each with much less difficulty than in most plays, the scenes being far more independent of each other.

139. There remains a third method, to take an incident from a story and dramatize it. This has the great advantage of providing you with plot and characters and sometimes part of the dialogue, though very considerable changes must be made, for a play is a vastly different thing from a narrative. You should have no difficulty in finding material. Dickens's novels have always been the happy hunting-ground of the adapter of " Scenes from the Great Novelists." Scott, Bulwer Lytton, Stevenson, Kipling, Conan Doyle, and W. W. Jacobs may be plundered equally well. (Copyright work must not be used outside the class-room or reading-circle unless special permission is obtained from the owner.) A

number of books in this series are very useful. *Pattern Plays*, by E. C. Oakden and Mary Sturt, contains stories, plays made from these stories, and further stories to be made into plays, with valuable hints on dramatization. *A Book of Escapes* and *The Path of the King*, by John Buchan, are treasure-houses of short, exciting incidents, and the non-copyright books include *The Arabian Nights*, Kingsley's *The Heroes*, *Scenes from " Quentin Durward,"* and the stories in Sir Henry Newbolt's *The Greenwood.*

Whether you borrow your plot, or invent it, you will be well advised to begin by writing a scenario, that is, a brief outline of your projected play.

140. Write scenarios of *Riders to the Sea* and *The Poetasters of Ispahan*, giving only the outline of the plot, and then study the way in which the story is developed in action and dialogue.

141. In most types of play, characterization is of very great importance. Good characterization can be based only upon thoughtful, sympathetic observation of the people whom you meet. The characters in your play must be different from each other and from you, and the differences will appear in their attitudes towards each other and towards what is happening, in their actions, their opinions, and their modes of speech. A simple and obvious method of differentiating a character is to make him speak in dialect (if you know one) or in bad English. Self-important people use formal, and sometimes affected, modes of speech ; a talkative, shallow man may gabble on while every one else is awed into silence, and thereby make their silence more impressive ; a coward will meet a sudden danger in a very different way from a brave man ; and so on. Moreover, the characters must be fairly consistent, and if any changes are to appear in them the audience must be carefully prepared in advance. If one of your persons suddenly does something which belies his whole character, merely in order to make your plot work out, then your play will be a failure. If, for example, your unselfish man is going to act selfishly in a particular instance—then the motives and circumstances which work the change in him must be carefully and convincingly shown. Make your characters human. The entirely faultless hero and the entirely fiendish villain

belong to melodrama, not to real life. And let their doings be human too, not superhuman. We all know the hero who is invariably lassoed from an aeroplane, just as the howling redskins set fire to the brushwood piled around him, and after a few chapters of similar events we wish he would get killed for a change. Leave him to " blood and thunder " stories and American films, and make your hero a human being in whom the audience will be interested.

142. Examine carefully the ways in which the characters are differentiated in *Riders to the Sea*, *Allison's Lad*, or *The Old Bull*, and describe the dramatist's methods.

143. Describe the features and general appearance of the Convict in *The Bishop's Candlesticks*, Burbage in *The Rehearsal*, and the Englishwoman in *The Little Man*, as you imagine them from the suggestions in the play.

144. A one-act play should have a beginning, a middle, and an end. This piece of advice is necessary, because many first plays by young writers do not possess any of these desirable things. The structure of several of the plays in this book may be studied very profitably. *Riders to the Sea* is a masterpiece of construction, and all the more so because its art is so successfully concealed, the skeleton so completely covered by the living flesh. The craftsmanship of *Allison's Lad* is excellent too, though it is more apparent and seems to be more laboured, and so is that of *The Little Man*, and *The Philosopher of Butterbiggins*. These should be divided into Exposition, Complication, Climax, and Dénouement, or according to any good scheme of your own.

145. In the Exposition the situation is explained, the characters are introduced, and action which happened before the play began is made known. What makes the expositions of *The Little Man* and *The Poetasters* unique in this book ? What methods are used, in these and in other plays, to take the audience's attention quickly and to make the giving of information natural ?

146. In the Complication the solution of the dramatic situation is made more difficult by the introduction of fresh factors, and suspense and interest are heightened. Exposition and Complication sometimes overlap. Do they do so in any play in this collection ?

147. At the Climax the play reaches its highest level of emotion. There may be more than one—minor climaxes followed by the major climax : find these, if they are to be found, in *Allison's Lad* and *Riders to the Sea.*

148. A Climax may be an inner or an outer one, corresponding to inner or outer conflict, or both combined. (See section 113.) Find examples in any of the plays in the book.

149. The Dénouement, or final unravelling of the plot, follows closely upon the climax in most one-act plays. Sometimes the climax and dénouement come together a moment before the curtain falls.

150. A thorough way of getting to understand the construction of a one-act play is to study every action and every speech, to find out why the author put it in.

151. Do not forget the elements of suspense and surprise. There is a story that Lord Dunsany has had only one lesson in play-writing, given him by Mr. W. B. Yeats : " Surprise . . . is what is necessary. Surprise, and then more surprise, and that is all." But Lord Dunsany has given himself many other lessons since.

152. Climaxes might be divided into those which involve surprise and those which fulfil expectation.

153. The importance of dialogue is very clear. A very important point, emphasized by Mr. Percival Wilde, is that dialogue does not usually develop the main line of thought from A to B to C to D to E and so on, but, say, from A to C to D to E to B to C to X to E to F to G to Y to C, etc.—doubling back, leaping forward, repeating important ideas and enlarging upon them, and sometimes bringing in ideas which are not strictly relevant, but create atmosphere, or reveal character, or give the illusion of real life. Study any passage of dialogue which appeals to you and see how far this applies to it.

154. The ideal to be aimed at in all prose-dialogue is that so vigorously described by Synge in his preface to *The Playboy of the Western World,* quoted on page 215. " Every speech as fully flavoured as a nut or apple . . ." and every speech characteristic of the speaker.

155. Important as it often is that the dialogue should *appear* to be quite natural, it can never copy exactly the conversation of real life. Like the other arts, drama does not merely copy life ; it selects and arranges the raw

material which life provides, in order to re-create and interpret.

Now:

156. Write the scenario only of the play you have projected.

157. Write an exact word-picture of the setting of the play.

158. Write a detailed description of the characters, the features, the dress, and the bearing of the people in your play.

159. Write your one-act play.

160. " I cautiously bought a book about how to write plays (there are many of them) in order to see whether Mr. Chapin wrote his properly.    But the book was so learned, and the author knew so much, and the subject when studied grew so difficult, that I hurriedly abandoned my inquiry. . . . Mr. Chapin certainly breaks most of the rules laid down in the early chapters of the guide-book, but breaks them so agreeably that one feels he had unconsciously found a better way for himself. . . . Perhaps this is merely his masterly cunning, and he has skilfully removed the ladders by which he climbed, but I scarcely think so.   I think he was the ' born dramatist,' who did not know how it was done but could do it."— J. M. BARRIE.

# ACTING NOTES

THESE brief notes on the plays in this collection are intended for those who know little or nothing of the art of dramatic production. There are several excellent books for the amateur, which teach as much as it is possible to teach of any art in a book, and it is not proposed to write a complete guide in this limited space, but to attempt instead what is rarely given—an account of the production of a particular play—*The Rehearsal*. The notes on the other plays, suggestive, not exhaustive, will be merely supplements to this account.

## THE REHEARSAL

We will assume that this play has been chosen because it can be cast fairly well from the actors available, offers a larger number of parts than is usual in a one-act play, is simple and inexpensive to dress and stage, and, most important of all, it is worth doing. (For some societies it will have the further attraction that all the characters are men, though one can imagine it performed well by a company of girls.)

*The Producer.*—When the society has organized its activities and finances (see the books recommended on page 245), the producer must set to work.

The producer is to the play, what the conductor is to the orchestra. He is responsible for the artistic harmony and unity of the play in all its details. He must have the power of final decision in all matters affecting this artistic harmony, and upon his tact and energy and enthusiasm, his knowledge and imagination, his willingness to experiment and learn, the success of the play will depend to a very large extent.

*Casting* is the first problem, whether it is done by a

small committee or by the producer alone. In the case of untried actors, the best plan is to begin with auditions (trial readings), at which the candidates for parts can read in turn various characters in *The Rehearsal*. The casting authority can then decide from voice, manner, and apparent acting potentialities, how the play is to be cast. Shakespeare is most important, of course. The actor who takes this part must be chosen primarily for his ability to make the speech " To-morrow and to-morrow . . ." beautiful and impressive, and he should also have a good presence and a face which can be made up to resemble somewhat the best-known pictures of the dramatist—the " Flower " portrait or the Droeshout engraving. Burbage must be able to make himself fussy, self-important, and irritable, and Hughes should not be stout and gruff ! The other characters are so lightly drawn that acting ability is the first and almost the only consideration. If under-studies can be appointed, so much the better ; they are a valuable insurance against disaster, if Shakespeare breaks his leg and the Witches develop measles on the day before the performance. Some societies choose two casts, which work quite inde-pendently of each other and are responsible for alternate performances.

*Permission to perform the play* should now be secured, and this must always be done before rehearsals begin, because some plays are not available for amateurs. (All the plays in this collection are available.) For *The Rehearsal*, application must be made to the author's agents, The Collection Bureau, The Society of Authors, 11 Gower Street, London, W.C.1. The royalty is one guinea for each public performance. (In case of doubt as to whether a performance is public or private, inquiries should be made of the British Drama League, or the dramatic agents concerned.) The society is bound in honour to pay the royalty, which is in many cases the chief source of the dramatist's income, and is simply a payment for the right to use his property. A dramatist should never be asked to waive the royalty because the performance is in aid of charity, because he prefers to choose for himself the charities to which he is to contri-bute. (Such performances are good for charity and bad for amateur drama, since they suggest that the latter is not on its own account worth paying to see.)    An increasing number of dramatists, however, accept percentage royalties instead of fixed fees.    (Inquire of the British Drama League.)

*Business arrangements*, such as booking a hall, advertising the play, and distributing tickets, should be made well in advance.    (*The Rehearsal* will obviously not make a complete programme by itself.)    Schools and some other educational institutions may get exemption from the Entertainment Tax, by applying on the Form E.D. 23, which can be obtained from the local Customs and Excise Office.

*The Stage.*—There is a great deal to be said for the stage simply set with screens or hung with curtains.    (See the books by Mr. Barrett Clark and Mr. Harold Ridge.) At least for those amateurs with no stage of their own, scenery is usually an expense and trouble out of all proportion to its worth, and most amateur scenery is artistically inferior to curtains.    In addition to the books cited, much help may be obtained from the chapter on " Stage-Setting " in *Shakespeare for Community Players,* by Roy Mitchell.    (Dent and Co., 6s.)

For *The Rehearsal* no better background is needed than plain dark curtains well hung.    These have the great advantages that they do not distract the eye, and that the movements of the actors show clearly against them.

*Stage Furniture and Properties.*—As soon as he can the producer should draw up a list of his requirements under these headings, for the benefit of the stage manager and others concerned in providing them.

In *The Rehearsal* the only furniture we need is a portable and rickety set of steps, and even for these we can substitute three or four stools piled upon each other, if we make a slight alteration in the dialogue.    The properties consist of several scrips for the players (sheets of white paper, scribbled over), and two swords, very obviously wooden, for the duel.    Macduff should be made responsible for taking the swords on the stage, and the players who need them made responsible for the scrips.

*Lighting* is very simple in this play, since only white light is needed and there are no changes.    The play can be given in daylight on an open stage, or even in the open air.

*Dresses* for an Elizabethan play are fairly easy to make. A ruff needs a strip of white book-muslin, about nine inches wide and five yards long, and demands more patience than skill in the construction. A waistcoat makes a good foundation for a doublet—ladies' stockings will do for hose, and gymnasium or dancing shoes, with rosettes, for the footwear. Full instructions for making these and all other Shakespearean dresses are given in *The Bankside Costume Book*, by M. Stone. (Wells Gardner, Darton, and Co., 3s.) Those who wish to hire costumes may get them from the Village Drama Society (see page 246) at very low charges; or from a theatrical costumier from about 7s. 6d. to 15s. each.

*Rehearsal.*—While all these arrangements are being made, rehearsals of the play must begin, and these the producer controls.

The aim of the producer should be to present to the audience as full and clearly, as beautifully or as humorously as possible, what it is that the dramatist has to say to them ; every detail of acting, setting, and lighting should be regulated to this end. So the first thing to do is to study the play.

It will be seen that *The Rehearsal* depends for its effect upon the contrast between the tragic note of Shakespeare's speech, "To-morrow and to-morrow . . ." and the comedy of the actors fretting and fuming, as well as upon the way in which the one suggests the other. The play, therefore, has to be "worked" to bring out this connection and contrast, besides the full humour of the comedy and the full beauty of the poetry.

The stage directions given in the text are inadequate for production, so they must be supplemented. Some producers work out every detail of movement, grouping, and gesture with a model stage and puppets, before they begin rehearsing ; others decide only upon the main outlines and fill in the details with the actors. The producer must work out his own artistic salvation in this as in many other matters, but at least he must go to the first rehearsal with entrances and exits and important stage movements clear in his mind and on his scrip. Stage-plans, showing the positions of the characters at important points in the action, are a great help to the beginner.

We may decide as follows. If there is no front curtain, Shakespeare, Producer, Stage Manager, Banquo, Macduff, and the three witches troop on from the right (the audience's right), all except Shakespeare talking together, and take up these positions, or take them up in silence before the curtain rises. Shakespeare is on the extreme left, well down stage,* and the Stage Manager and Producer are on the extreme right, down stage. Macduff and Banquo stand at left centre, and the witches at centre back, so that the middle of the stage is clear, with the steps to the left of this open space. †

Shakespeare stands silent and motionless (he must stand quite still, not fidget), watching the actors, and makes no sign until he checks Mr. Hughes (page 48). This aloofness gives him slowly increasing dignity, by comparison with the petty squabbles of the others, and leads up effectively to his " big " speech.

It is a good plan for the Producer and the Stage Manager to talk in dumb show for a second or two, till the preliminary whispering and rustling of the audience have died down. During their dialogue the other actors listen and whisper among themselves. The witches come forward when they " suppose they can go," Banquo joins them during his first speech, and when the Producer says, " Now, Act V. . . ." (in a tone approaching command), they all turn away to their places except the First Witch. The last-named takes the centre of the stage to read the waiting gentlewoman's part—and so on. All the important stage movements should be marked on the " prompt copy " of the play. The fight must be exactly rehearsed, not left as a haphazard, impromptu affair.

There should be a slow crescendo of restrained exasperation throughout the play, until Shakespeare reads, " To-morrow and to-morrow . . ." This should be received in spellbound silence by all the others, there

---

\* " Down stage " means towards the audience, and " up stage " away from them—a reminder that stages used to be built sloping up towards the back.

† For an example of main stage movements worked out for a whole play, see the Acting Notes to *The Old Bull*.

should be a second's silence after the speech, and then the exasperation should burst out unrestrained, with the actors crowding in upon the Stage Manager and Producer, until they give up in despair and stride out, left, with the others crowding after them and muttering.

At the first rehearsal the only thing for the actors to do is " read for position "—reading their parts without care for expression, and simply learning their movements. After this the actors should make themselves word-perfect in their parts as quickly as they can : it is a mistake for actors, especially if they are young and inexperienced, to be set to learn their parts before rehearsals begin.

The play then has to be built up at successive rehearsals—twenty or more may be necessary—and when it is in mechanically good " going order " the Producer can work for " atmosphere," for all those little subtilties of intonation and movement which make the supreme difference between a living work of art and a mechanical performance.

The actors, as well as the Producer, will have much to learn, and the latter should be prepared to give training in speech and movement if it is needed. Every word of the play must be audible to the people in the back row of the audience, and this is a question not of shouting, but of correct pitch and clear enunciation. Speech should normally be as pleasant and natural as possible, without any " elocution for elocution's sake." In *The Rehearsal* there must be a clear distinction between the actors' tones when they are speaking in their own characters, and when they are rehearsing *Macbeth*. The Shakespearean lines should be given in tones of slightly exaggerated declamation.

Actors must speak to the front when they can reasonably do so ; avoid passing in front of any one who is speaking ; avoid distracting attention from him ; stand still, when they do stand still, without being stiff and without shuffling about ; and move definitely when they do move. All movements must be natural or made to appear natural, not merely obvious devices for " changing the picture." Actors standing in the background of *The Rehearsal* should lounge and occasionally whisper.

The Producer should do everything possible to encourage players to " think themselves into " their parts, to understand as fully as they can what they are doing and saying and feeling, and to act all the time they are on the stage, not merely while they are speaking. And they must learn to take their cues very promptly, so that there are no little gaps in the play between speeches. Every actor should understand the entire play, and regard its success as a whole as a much more important thing than his individual success in his own part ; though he must realize that his own part, however small, is vital to the whole.

*The Dress Rehearsal* should be a day or two days before the performance, and should be as much like a performance as possible, with full lighting, stage-setting, dresses, and make-up, and a small, select audience if desired. The Producer should let the rehearsal go through without interruption or alteration, if these can possibly be avoided ; but he may give a few words of final advice to the cast— especially to keep the play going whatever happens in performance. It is astonishing what audiences will not notice, if the players do not hesitate. If they are to take a " final curtain " this should be rehearsed, or it will almost certainly be muddled.

There is no need for any one to worry if the dress rehearsal is altogether miserable and depressing. Dress rehearsals often are ; but if the play has been faithfully rehearsed it will spring into full life in the performance.

*Make-up* for *The Rehearsal* need not be complete (that is, covering the whole face, neck, and ears) unless the stage lighting is high. A little rouge on the cheeks and darkening of the brows should be all the grease-paint needed, and all the actors (except Mr. Hughes) should have the familiar Elizabethan moustache and short-pointed beard—made of crêpe-hair " fluffed out," stuck on with spirit-gum, and then trimmed. At the dress rehearsal all make-up (and dresses) should be carefully scrutinized from the hall. Crêpe-hair is removed with methylated spirits, and grease-paint with coco-butter or vaseline. The fascinating art of make-up is dealt with in the books recommended on page 245.

*The Programme* should give the names of the actors in the order in which they appear or speak. This avoids any question as to precedence, and is an aid to the audience in identifying characters.

Besides giving the scene and date of *The Rehearsal*, it may be advisable to add a note that women's parts were played by youths on the Elizabethan stage, or the audience may be sadly puzzled at the appearance of Lady Macbeth and the witches in male costume.

*The Performance.*—The Producer's responsibility ends, in theory, with the dress rehearsal, when it passes to the Stage Manager, who is responsible for the stage setting, furniture, properties, and so on. But the Producer will be well advised to remain in the wings to deal with any emergency, and help keep the cast in good spirits. They may be comforted with the information that many experienced professional actors are always nervous before they go on! *The Rehearsal* takes about twenty minutes in performance.

The chief essentials for an artistic production are good team-work, imagination, enthusiasm, loyalty, and "an infinite capacity for taking pains." It will be noticed that wealth is not included. One of the most delightful things about amateur dramatic work is the fine results which may be obtained with slender means.

## THE BISHOP'S CANDLESTICKS

The fee for each representation of this play by amateurs is fifteen shillings, payable in advance to Messrs. Samuel French, Limited, 26 Southampton Street, Strand, London, W.C.2, or their authorized representatives, who, upon payment of the fee, will send a written permission for performances to take place. No public performance may be given unless this written permission has first been obtained. The play takes about thirty minutes in performance. The " right " and " left " of the stage directions are those of the actors, not of the audience. The stage plan is on page 254.

Like all the other plays in this book, except perhaps *The Little Man* and *Riders to the Sea*, this play may very well be performed on a curtained stage ; but curtains do not preclude the use of a " practical " window and door, which are particularly desirable for this play and not difficult to construct. Above and below the window the rectangular wooden framework which contains it should be covered with pieces of the material of which the stage curtains are made. Glass is not necessary. The lattice-work of the window can be made of black tape stretched from side to side of the window frame. For both window and door a plain backcloth, of black or dark blue, is better than a " winter wood scene " if the stage is curtained. Unless the setting has to be changed immediately before or after the play, it is best to have the frames for the door and window screwed securely to the stage and (where possible) to a beam above. When the change is to, or from, a plain curtain background, it is easy to arrange the curtains to draw across the window and door. In any case it is usually very convenient to hang the door upon "lift-on " hinges, so that it can be moved separately. It is a great advantage to dispense with a crossbar at the bottom of the door whenever possible, for inexperienced actors have a way of tripping over it, in the performance if not in the rehearsals. The framework of both door and window must be solid enough not to quiver violently —to the amusement of the audience—when they are touched.

The doors to right and left can be simply openings in the curtains. Almost any solid oak furniture, except Jacobean, will do for the stage. (Happy is the dramatic society which is on good terms with the local dealers in antique furniture !) The hooded fireplace,* with a broad shelf, can be constructed without much difficulty, and should be made to stand against the curtains without any fixing. It may be necessary to raise the " hearth " above the stage level, so that the audience can see the " fire," which consists of two firedogs (of wood, painted black), with sticks and logs nailed across them as naturally as possible, and in the middle a wire cage covered with red paper, over an electric light bulb, preferably red.

This play especially needs simple and sincere acting, and the producer should work for this, and make sure that every player understands thoroughly the character he is representing. If there is any trace of sentimentality, or any striving after theatrical effect, or any playing to

---

* See the Acting Notes to *The Philosopher of Butterbiggins*.

the audience ;—if the bishop is sanctimonious and pleased with himself, and the Convict whines about his sufferings, expecting or desiring pity, instead of remaining " a wild beast " until nearly the end—then the play will be ruined.

## THE PHILOSOPHER OF BUTTERBIGGINS

All applications for permission to perform this play must be addressed to Messrs. Samuel French, Limited, 26 Southampton Street, Strand, London, W.C.2, or their authorized representatives.   The fee for each and every representation of the play by amateurs is one guinea. This sum is payable in advance, and no performance may take place unless a written permission has first been obtained.

This play takes about thirty minutes in performance.

It is fairly obvious that the dark curtains recommended for *The Rehearsal* and *The Bishop's Candlesticks* will not do for this play ;  they would be much too rich in effect. The stage may be hung with curtains of hessian or some similar material ;  or set with screens " distempered a brickish red " ;  or a realistic " box-set " may be made— a room complete except for the " fourth wall," through which the audience views it, and constructed to the dramatist's description.   Such a set would be a wooden framework covered with distempered canvas or old newspapers.

The bare essentials, however, are a plain background, a deal table, a few chairs, and a fireplace.   Even the last might be omitted, but at a considerable loss.   A small dramatic society should have several fireplaces, self-contained, and made to stand by themselves—say, a modern drawing-room fireplace, a kitchen grate, and a wide antique-looking fireplace which will do equally well for the fourteenth or the eighteenth century, and would serve very well, for example, for *The Bishop's Candlesticks*.   These fireplaces, stood against screens or scenery or curtains, can be used again and again.   Red paper and an electric light globe will do for the basis of any fire, and if flames are specially desired, no doubt some member of the company will enjoy constructing them with strips of silk, kept in motion by a small, *silent* electric fan, concealed in the fire.

The substitution of an oil lamp for the gas removes the only real difficulty in staging *The Philosopher of Butterbiggins*. If the fading daylight can be represented with the help of a dimmer switch, so much the better.

The play demands natural production and acting—not easy for amateurs—but the chief difficulty for many will be the dialect. The music of good Scots is too beautiful to be travestied by any clumsy theatrical imitation ; the best advice to actors who cannot speak as a true Scotsman would seems to be not to attempt the play.

## THE PRICE OF COAL

The fee for every representation of this play by amateurs is one guinea, payable in advance to Messrs. Samuel French, Limited. (See *The Bishop's Candlesticks*.)

The play takes about thirty minutes in performance.

If scenery is not attempted, the best background for this play is curtains of plain hessian or some similar material, to give the impression of bareness and poverty. The lighting should be low at first to give the chilly atmosphere of the early morning, and increased as the play goes on. It would be an advantage to have a door, of course, but if this is difficult the door can be an imaginary one " off "—in which case it should be heard when it is shut and locked, and Polly should take care that the audience sees the key. There should be no difficulty in borrowing or improvising dresses and furniture. (Jack's clothes must be thoroughly blackened, not slightly soiled !) An oil lamp, or candles, can be substituted for gas. If the kettle is filled with *hot* water, there will be no fear of its not boiling quickly enough on the oil-stove—though Mary's silent " business " at the beginning, preparing Jack's lunch, etc., should not be scamped, for it contributes a good deal to the " atmosphere " of the play : it needs careful and detailed rehearsal. A real fire is almost certain to be impossible, though if there is a stove it can be cleared of ashes, and the fire laid, but abandoned

for the oil stove.   Some slight alterations in the dialogue
will enable this difficulty to be avoided.

The bell or gong used for the alarm must have a deep
warning note :  any resemblance to a muffin bell or a tin
tray (or the school bell) will be fatal !

The most important problem, that of the dialect, remains to be mentioned.   It is not nearly so difficult as it
may appear at first sight, even to players in the south of
England.   It is not advisable to attempt the play without
dialect, or for actors who do not speak " Lancashire " to
attempt to do so unless they have expert coaching ;  but
the play has already been translated into the dialect of
Lanarkshire, and there is no reason why it should not be
given in that of any coalfield, or even—in case of necessity—in any provincial dialect.

## ALLISON'S LAD

For permission to produce this play application must
be made to Mr. R. Golding Bright, 20 Green Street,
Leicester Square, London.   The royalty is one guinea.

The play takes about thirty minutes in performance.

Dramatic societies which have difficulty in filling
women's parts, and boy's schools in particular, should be
grateful to Miss Dix for having written that very rare
thing—a good one-act tragedy in which all the characters
are men.   Moreover, it is exceptionally easy to stage,
and its stagecraft is so good that one feels it will almost
" play itself " if the actors have sincere tragic feeling.   It
must be faithfully rehearsed, however, to guard against
any mistake or hesitation which would break the emotional tension ;  faults of this kind are much more serious
in tragedy than in comedy, and in a short play than a
long one.   The actors who play Strickland and Winwood
should have some poetry in them, and be sufficiently in
sympathy to act well together.   It is only by enthusiasm,
sincerity, and patient hard work that the amateur can
counterbalance to some extent his inevitable inferiority
in technique to the professional actor.

Dark curtains and simple oak furniture, and a fireplace
if possible, are all that is needed for the stage.   Low
lighting is essential, to give the " two o'clock in the

morning " atmosphere, and in a small hall it may be possible to dispense with all lighting except a number of candles on the stage.

## THE OLD BULL

The fee for each and every representation of this play by amateurs is one guinea, payable in advance to Messrs. Samuel French, Limited, or their authorized representatives. No public performance may be given unless this written permission has first been obtained.

The play takes about thirty minutes in performance.

The description of the Grange kitchen may dismay the producer as much as it would gladden the American, but though such an elaborate setting would make an excellent background for the play, it can be discarded without hesitation if simplicity is desired. In fact, the play can very well be given in daylight on a curtained stage or in the open air, with no other furniture than a table (centre), three chairs (behind and on either side of the table), and a dresser (right) ; and two entrances, left and right.

If this setting is adopted, the fireplace being dispensed with, it is suggested that the following stage movements should be followed. Sarah enters from the left (audience's left) with a bottle of " sherry " (ginger ale ?), and three wine-glasses on a tray. She crosses to the dresser on the right, sets down the tray, takes a duster from a drawer, and polishes the glasses during the first part of her dialogue with Bones, who also enters from the left and stands at left centre. They keep these positions until Bones says, " I know which I'd sooner have in the old gentleman's place," when Sarah comes to the back of the right-hand chair as she " puts her fingers to her lips," and Bones moves a step or two nearer. When James enters, from the left, he crosses to the table, speaking as he does so, and sits in the chair behind the table, full face to the audience, puts his hat on the chair against which Sarah is leaning, and makes a half-hearted attempt, soon abandoned, to mend the whip he is carrying. Bones goes out, left, and Sarah moves nearer to James, speaking confidentially till she hears or sees Charles approach, when she goes out quickly, right, with her head in the air. James, who has rested his head on his right hand while he was talking to Sarah, ignores Charles, who comes down stage, left, puts his left foot on the chair and surveys his brother in silent derision for a moment before " giving James a poke with his riding-whip." Charles remains in this position until he sees the sherry, when he walks across to the dresser, right, talking about Uncle William as he goes. Having filled his glass, he lounges against the dresser, talking, until he says, " Perhaps you expected to be left in one of the farms," when he crosses to the chair, right, where Sarah stood, and leans across the back of it, putting his second glass of wine on the table. James starts up, *away from* Charles, at " You won't sack Bones ? " and the two face each other thus until Sarah enters, right, with her message. She stands between them, but a little " up stage of them," looking from one to the other. When told to go, James goes with obvious reluctance.

Charles then takes James's hat from the chair against which he is leaning, throws it on the floor and drops into the chair. Sarah moves round the back of the table until she is nearly at the opposite end, and then questions Charles, until she hurries out, right, to see about the yew. Charles gets a third glass of sherry, and sits down in the same chair. Bones enters left, and stands at left centre as before. When Sarah runs in, crying, " It's down," she stands behind the centre chair, and both she and Bones close in on Charles when they are all speaking at once. " At the height of the tumult " William Smithson enters, left, and, standing on the threshold, " takes command of the situation." After Charles has said, " I will if they don't shut up," William goes to the chair behind the table, and says, " Now," as he sits down. James, who has followed William in, remains in the background trying to quieten Sarah and Bones, until he says, " It's a poor lookout for me then, uncle," when he comes forward and takes the one empty chair, left, in order to join in the discussion. The position is now as follows : seated, Uncle William in the middle, Charles at the right end of the table, and James at the left ; standing, Sarah, between William and James, but a couple of paces back, and Bones a little to the left of James.

From this point the movements are sufficiently indicated by the stage directions in the text. At the end,

Bones enters from the left and must come well down stage, left. All the others make an impulsive movement towards him as he speaks. If there is no front curtain, effective exits can be arranged as follows. After Sarah's last speech, Charles stamps off, right, speechless with anger. Bones goes out, left, as he makes his last speech, and Sarah and James follow him. Uncle William, chuckling, pours himself out a glass of sherry, drinks it with relish, laughs heartily, with a glance after Charles, and then goes out left.

There is only one small problem—the sound of the yew falling. This can be imitated behind the scenes by breaking a number of boughs which have been sawn half-through—and this needs rehearsal—or omitted entirely, without loss.

It will be seen that all the movements outlined above are simple and natural. The play must be made as realistic as possible—the more so because it is rather too " well made." The aim of the producer should be to make it go at the speed and in the manner of real life, and when this is done it is a very amusing play. It acts much better than it reads, and its acting quality will be found to advance steadily during rehearsal if the actors think out their characterization.

All of them, and Bones in particular, should speak more slowly than townsfolk do. Dialect need be only slightly suggested, except in the case of Bones, and is left to the actors. It is a good plan to make James rather unattractive, by accentuating the weakness of character which Mr. Gilbert implies in him, so that the play is not too obviously the story of the bad elder brother and the good younger brother, the motive of innumerable legends and tales all the world over.


## THE LITTLE MAN

For permission to perform this play application must be made to the Collection Bureau, The Incorporated Society of Authors, 11 Gower Street, London, W.C.1.

In performance the play takes about forty minutes, excluding intervals.

At first sight the railway carriage setting may appear

as impossible for a small amateur stage as the other settings are easy. But the producer need not be dismayed. He should write to the British Drama League, which offers a solution of the difficulty ; or simply set the stage as a narrow room, with two long seats, by using screens or curtains to reduce the proscenium opening, and allow the audience to imagine a railway carriage. This is much more likely to be an artistic success than any ingenious and elaborate piece of stage trickery, to which the audience would give more attention than to the play itself, in a very natural curiosity as to how it was done ! Over-emphasized realism always defeats its own end.

The timely halo provided by the sanitary machine presents another problem. If it is too difficult, then the ray of sunlight alone will do, and a powerful electric bulb or acetylene lamp, with a horn-shaped reflector of tin or cardboard, will provide the ray if there is no limelight available.

The play needs to go briskly, without hitch or hesitation. All the characters should be over-accentuated a little, the American must be *very* American, and the large doll used for the baby must not be so obviously a doll as dolls usually are on the amateur stage.

## THE POETASTERS OF ISPAHAN

Application for permission to give amateur performances of this play should be made to Mr. A. D. Peters, Literary Agent, 20 Essex Street, Strand, W.C.2. The fee for performances by *school* dramatic societies is one guinea ; others should inquire of Mr. Peters.

The play takes about forty-five minutes in performance.

One of the producer's chief aims in this play must be to see that the farce does not overwhelm the poetry, or the play will lose half its appeal. Hallaj, in particular, must be able to speak verse well, with sentiment which does not lapse into sentimentality, and must not be afraid to stand still and speak quietly. Good lighting with dimmer switches contributes greatly to the play, but if desired it can be given in daylight, on an open stage or in the open air. A simple and effective front curtain can be arranged by sending on two negro slaves, to support a light curtain between two spears, while the stage is set and Hallaj takes his place.

Silvermoon should be a little darker-skinned than an English girl ; the slaves need black skin-tights and negro make-up ; the make-up for the remainder is simply ruddy rouge powder, with beards of various shapes and shades.

## RIDERS TO THE SEA

For permission to give amateur performances of this play application must be made to Messrs. Samuel French, Limited, or their authorized representatives. The fee for each and every performance is one guinea, payable in advance.

The play takes about thirty minutes in performance.

As Mr. G. K. Chesterton has pointed out, if a thing is worth doing at all, it is worth doing badly. Amateur actors who attempt *Riders to the Sea*, believing in the play and sensitive to its tragedy and poetry, will do so with joy and profit to themselves and probably to their audience. At least they will realize that failure with such a play as this is worth a great deal more to every one concerned than easy success with a play that is essentially worthless.

## BOOKS FOR ACTOR AND PRODUCER

*A List of Plays for Young Players.* Village Drama Society. (To be published in 1926 or early in 1927.)

This list, compiled by the Society's Junior Plays Committee, contains the titles of over two hundred plays, suitable for performance by players of all ages under eighteen, and carefully selected, classified, and annotated. The selection ranges from nursery-rhyme playlets to the work of Shaw, Molière, and Euripides. Bibliographies and indexes.

*How to Produce Amateur Plays.* Barrett H. Clark. Harrap, 5s.

A practical book which covers the whole ground from organization and rehearsal to staging and make-up. Illustrated.

*Play Production for Everyone.*  Monica Ewer.  Labour
    Publishing Co., 3s. 6d. and 2s. 6d.

Briefer than Barrett H. Clark's book, but very useful;
stimulating and suggestive.

*Stage Lighting for " Little " Theatres.*  C. Harold Ridge.
    Heffer, 5s.

Every dramatic society should possess this book.  For
amateurs with a small stage and limited resources, lighting is the most artistic and most easily available aid in
production.


## DRAMATIC ORGANIZATIONS

*The British Drama League*, 8 Adelphi Terrace, London,
W.C.2.

*The Village Drama Society*, 15 Peckham Road, Cam-
berwell, London, S.E.5.

All amateurs will find it worth while to get into touch
with these organizations.  The latter gives special attention to the needs of village and school societies.

# APPENDIX

## THE PROCEDURE FOR A MOCK TRIAL

A MOCK TRIAL is a form of dramatic entertainment which can be made interesting, amusing, and instructive at the same time. Most dramatic societies will find it worth while to attempt such a trial occasionally, and since it is easier to stage and needs less rehearsal than a play, while providing much more scope for invention, it can be arranged in the schoolroom or the village hall with the expenditure of little time and, if desired, no money. But it must be arranged. The impromptu mock trial is very rarely a success.

The " crime " should be " discovered " some time in advance—though the " prisoner " must certainly be allowed out on bail !—the most important details of the story decided, and the players instructed in their various parts. If a public performance is to be given, at least one rehearsal is necessary. Speeches, evidence, etc., need not be learned word for word, but each player must know the main facts and ideas which he is to contribute to the progress of the trial, and in most cases notes may be used unobtrusively. Judge and Counsel can have this book open in front of them, with a full " plan " of the trial.

If the whole plot can be invented by the leading players or the organizer, so much the better. If not, it may be based upon a trial in a novel, such as that of Darnay in *A Tale of Two Cities* (for which eighteenth-century costume is needed) or the familiar case of Bardell *v.* Pickwick in *The Pickwick Papers* (which can be given in an adaptation of modern dress). The stories of Sherlock Holmes and other detectives provide very useful material, but public performances based on these cannot be given without permission from the owners of the copyright. Boys and girls greatly enjoy inventing a new Sherlock Holmes mystery, and providing him with a dramatic entry, accompanied by excited witnesses, in the middle of the trial, when the (innocent) prisoner is in grave danger of being convicted by circumstantial evidence. The opportunity for useful classroom work need not be emphasized.

The summary of procedure given below is approximately that of an Assize Court. This is less familiar and more impressive than the ritual of the " Police Court," and the Assize deals with serious crimes which are suitable for a mock trial—such as arson, burglary, housebreaking, embezzlement, forgery, larceny, and making false coin and banknotes. It is suggested that a mock trial might be very profitably followed or preceded by some work on our legal system and the function of the various courts. The necessary information can be obtained from such books as Mr. F. Swann's *Primer of English Citizenship* (Longmans, Green, and Co.).

The Assize can be arranged simply or elaborately. Though the gilded coach and the javelin-men are not available for " the legal representative of the King," there should be little difficulty in arranging for trumpeters " off " (Boy Scouts with bugles ?) to announce the entry of a Judge resplendent in scarlet and ermine (flannelette and cotton-wool).

If a stage is available, so much the better, but in either case it is necessary to have a dais for the Judge, and advisable to have a lower one for the Clerks. Draped boxes or tables will do. (Dramatic societies will find it a good plan to buy a stock of butter boxes, which are cheap, strong, and portable, and excellent for a dais. For stage use they can be painted and built into a number of different properties.) Two black-boards, a small screen, or a draped towel-horse will do for the witness-box, and two long desks or forms for the Jury. The " bar " to which the prisoner is called can be a thin pole or brass rod lashed to two uprights—chairs will do.

The Judge wears a flowing scarlet robe trimmed with ermine ; the Clerk and Counsel wear university gowns, if available, with stiff collars (but no tie), and bands—

*i.e.* two narrow strips of white linen hanging from the collar in front. If uniforms can be borrowed or improvised for policemen and warders or wardresses, so much the better, but these are not so important. There should be as much variety as possible in the dress, make-up, and manner of the prisoner and witnesses, who can be of widely different ages, classes, and nationalities.

When everything is ready, and the jury and audience are seated, the Assize proceeds as follows :

[*Enter the* Usher.]

*Usher* [*proclaiming loudly*]. Oyez ! Oyez ! Oyez ! All manner of persons having aught to do before His Majesty the King and the Lords Justices of Assize draw near and give their attendance.

> [*Enter the* Clerk of Assize, *the* Counsel for the Prosecution, *the* Counsel for the Defence, *and the* Judge. *Every one present rises as the* Judge *enters, and remains standing until he has taken his seat.*
>
> *Enter the* Prisoner, *guarded* [*if a man*] *by two* Warders, *or* [*if a woman*] *by two* Wardresses.
>
> *Every one except the* Judge *rises when speaking.*]

*Clerk of Assize* [*rising and reading the charge*]. " John Doe is charged that on the 8th day of December 1926, at . . . in the County of . . . he did feloniously . . . against the peace of our Lord the King his crown and dignity." Prisoner at the Bar, you have heard the Charge. Do you plead Guilty or Not Guilty ?

*Prisoner.* Not Guilty.

*Clerk of Assize.* John Doe, the names I am about to call are those of the Jury who will try you. If you object to any of them, you must do so before they are sworn, and your objection will be heard.

> [*The members of the* Jury *rise. The* Clerk of Assize *reads the twelve names in full, the* Foreman's *first—e.g.* Thomas Henry Wilkinson, Frederick Jones, *etc.*
>
> *The* Prisoner *having made no objection,* * *the* Clerk *reads the words of the oath which the* Jury *are to take.*]

*Clerk of Assize.* You shall well and truly try the issue

---

* If he does object to any juryman it should be for some absurd reason.

joined between our Sovereign Lord the King and the Prisoner at the Bar whom you shall have in charge, and true verdict give according to the evidence.*

> [*As the last words of the oath are pronounced, the* Jury *raise their right hands, and then sit. The* Counsel for the Prosecution *rises.*]

*Counsel for Prosecution* outlines the crime of which he intends to prove the Prisoner guilty, and then announces the name of his first witness—*e.g.* William Warburton.

*Judge's Clerk* [*calling*]. William Warburton !

> [WILLIAM WARBURTON *enters, and goes into the witness-box. The* Judge's Clerk *gives him* [*and every witness who follows*] *a card on which the words of the oath are printed.*]

*William Warburton* [*reading the oath slowly and solemnly*]. † The evidence that I shall give between our Sovereign Lord the King and the Prisoner at the Bar shall be the truth, the whole truth, and nothing but the truth.†

*Counsel for Prosecution* proceeds to question the Witness, trying to elicit evidence which will show that the Prisoner is guilty. The Witness answers as clearly and briefly as possible, except when a touch of humour is desired.

> [*During the examination the* Judge *may ask questions on any point which he thinks needs explanation, for his own benefit or that of the audience. When the* Counsel for the Prosecution *has finished with the* Witness *he sits down and the* Counsel for the Defence *rises.*]

*Counsel for Defence* proceeds to cross-examine the Witness, with a view to weakening or disproving the evidence which he has given previously, and obtaining evidence in favour of the Prisoner.

> [*When* Counsel for the Defence *has finished, he sits, and* Counsel for the Prosecution *either asks further questions or gives the* Witness *leave to go. When this is given* Witness *leaves the box and takes a seat near by. Except when giving evidence no witness is allowed in court, but this rule need not be enforced.*]

---

* The words "so help you God" are here omitted.
† The words "I swear by Almighty God" and "so help me God" are here omitted.

[*When all* Witnesses for the Prosecution *have been heard :*]

*Counsel for Prosecution.* That is my case, my lord.
[*Sits down.*

*Counsel for Defence.* I propose to call the Prisoner to give evidence, my lord.

[Witnesses for the Defence *are then called, the* Prisoner *being the first.* (*He is not compelled to give evidence, but nearly always does so.*)]

Prisoner *is taken into the witness-box by a* Warder, *and is sworn as a witness. After being examined by* Counsel for the Defence *and cross-examined by* Counsel for the Prosecution, Prisoner *is taken back into the dock.*]

*Counsel for Defence* [*rising*] makes his longest and most important speech, beginning : " My Lord and Gentlemen of the Jury." He sums up all the evidence which tells in favour of the Prisoner, tries to discredit or refute (or passes over in silence) the evidence against him, refers to any past legal decisions which have bearing on the case, and does all in his power to influence the Jury in favour of the Prisoner by an eloquent appeal to their reason and their emotions. [*He sits.*

*Counsel for Prosecution* [*rising*] makes a similar speech on the other side. [*Sits.*

*Judge* [*remaining seated*]. " Gentlemen of the Jury, you have to decide whether the Prisoner on . . . did . . ." He then proceeds to give the Jury an impartial summing up of the facts which have been established by the evidence, drawing their attention to anything which he considers to be of special importance, and concludes, " Can you decide upon your verdict here, or do you wish to retire to consider it ? "

*Foreman,* after a brief consultation with the Jury, announces that they wish to retire, or that they do not.

[*If the* Jury *retire, the* Court *must wait until they have returned to their places ; but it is better if they can come to their decision (which must be unanimous) without retiring. When they have decided, the* Judge *proceeds at once.*]

*Judge* [*to* Foreman]. Are you agreed upon your verdict ?

*Foreman.* Yes, my Lord.

[*If he says that they have not been able to come to an*

*agreement, the* Judge *must announce that the case will be tried again at the next Assizes.*]

*Judge.* Do you find the Prisoner Guilty or Not Guilty ?

[*If the verdict is Not Guilty :*]

*Foreman.* Not Guilty, my Lord.

*Judge.* John Doe, I concur in the verdict. You leave the Court without a stain on your character.

[*If the verdict is Guilty ; or Guilty with Recommendation to Mercy :*]

*Foreman.* Guilty, my Lord, *or* Guilty, my Lord, with Recommendation to Mercy.

*Judge.* " Prisoner at the Bar, you have been found guilty of a grave offence, which . . ." He points out the evil results of the particular crime, and then, tempering his remarks and sentence accordingly if the Prisoner has been recommended to mercy, he concludes, " I sentence you to . . ." [The sentence for burglary should be two years' imprisonment or three or more years' penal servitude ; for arson, penal servitude ; for forgery, imprisonment with or without hard labour, or penal servitude. The shortest period of penal servitude which can be given is three years.]

[*If the* Prisoner *is Not Guilty, he is free to leave the Court ; if Guilty, he is escorted to his cell by the* Warders. *The Court then rises, the* Clerk of Assize, Counsel, *etc., leaving in the order in which they entered.*]

## RECORD OF A MOCK TRIAL

held by.................................on..........

The Judge . . . . ....................
Counsel for the Prosecution . ....................
Counsel for the Defence . . ....................
Clerk of Assize . . . ....................
Judge's Clerk . . . ....................
Usher . . . . ....................
Prisoner (            ) . . ....................
First Warder . . . ....................
Second Warder . . . ....................
Twelve Jurymen (their real names) :
       Foreman....................

..................... .....................
..................... .....................
..................... .....................
..................... .....................
..................... .....................

Witnesses :

..................... .....................
..................... .....................
..................... .....................
..................... .....................
..................... .....................

The Charge.....................................

The Verdict.....................................
The Sentence....................................

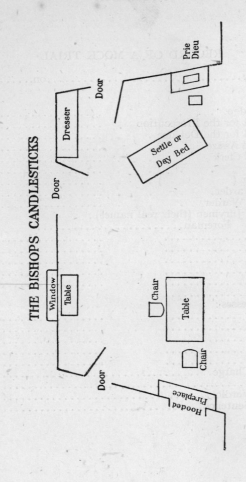

THE BISHOPS CANDLESTICKS

Window
Table
Door
Dresser
Door
Prie Dieu
Settle or Day Bed
Chair
Table
Chair
Door
Hooded Fireplace

PRINTED IN GREAT BRITAIN AT
THE PRESS OF THE PUBLISHERS.